I hope this book equips and inspires you with the tools to slay all the demons on your golf journey.

Love,
JMM

FROM HACK TO SCRATCH

By Joshua Medcalf

Golf is deceptively simple and endlessly complicated; it satisfies the soul and frustrates the intellect. It is at the same time rewarding and maddening—and it is without a doubt the greatest game mankind has ever invented.
—Arnold Palmer

TABLE OF CONTENTS

Chapter 1   Use Golf, Don't Let It Use You · 1
Chapter 2   You Can Do This · 4
Chapter 3   The Struggle · 9
Chapter 4   Tiger Woods at Torrey Pines · 14
Chapter 5   "You Gotta Meet Sam!" · 17
Chapter 6   All Hard Work Is Not Equal · 28
Chapter 7   State-Based Learning · 34
Chapter 8   Comfortable with Uncomfortability · · · · · · · · · · · · · · · · · 37
Chapter 9   The Club Championship · 42
Chapter 10 Twelve Feet and In · 72
Chapter 11 The Path to Mastery · 77
Chapter 12 When Are You at Your Best? · 79
Chapter 13 Performance Cue Card · 81
Chapter 14 Identity · 86
Chapter 15 The Perfectionism Myth · 87
Chapter 16 Rewiring Your Brain · 90
Chapter 17 How Do You Talk to Yourself? · 95
Chapter 18 Language Is a Filter to Meaning · 97
Chapter 19 New Scorecard · 101
Chapter 20 Forged in the Fire · 103
Chapter 21 Pound the Stone · 107
Thank You's · 110

CHAPTER 1

USE GOLF, DON'T LET IT USE YOU

I DON'T KNOW if you have ever felt like this, but man, Golf can beat the shit out of me. It can turn me into a monster of a human. It has used and abused me. Sometimes playing the game feels like being in an abusive relationship that I can't quit. I still revert back to bad patterns at times, but I have worked very hard at learning how to use golf, instead of letting it use and abuse me.

If you have ever heard me speak or read any of my other books you know the following story is my absolute favorite to tell, and I believe it has a lot to do with how I was able to become a scratch golfer. I never set out to achieve anything. I only focused on becoming the best I could be at golf. The achievements and results were simply byproducts of falling in love with the process.

There was once a little boy named John. He loved building as a kid, and he would build entire cities out of *Legos* and building blocks. When John became an adult, he finally had the opportunity to start building homes. Eventually his work became world famous due to his dedication to the process, his willingness to beat on his craft, and his tireless devotion to learning, even late into his career.

In time, though, John grew tired of building homes for other people. He had been building homes for over thirty years, and he was ready for the next phase of his life. He wanted to travel, play golf, and spend lots of time with his grandkids.

Soon after, he approached his boss and turned in his two weeks' notice.

"John," his boss said, "we are forever indebted to you for the magnificent work you have done for our company, and we are so grateful you have worked for us for so long. We have one favor to ask of you, though. Could you please build one more house? It is a very important house for a very important client, and everyone in the company agreed it needs your magic touch!"

John was frustrated. He would have to cancel two trips and postpone his new life, all for one house. He told his boss that he needed a day to think about it. After talking it over with his wife, he gave in.

"This is the very last one," he told his boss. "After this, I am done!"

While John had agreed with his *head*, his *heart* was no longer in it. He had always been very hands-on during the building process, eager to select the finest materials by hand and make sure every detail was diligently tended to.

This house was different.

He viewed it more as an obligation than an opportunity. He delegated much of the work, and things started slipping through the cracks. The house would be up to code, but it was obvious that it lacked the "wow" factor of John's other homes.

John knew in his heart that this home was far from his best work, but he was over it. He was ready to move on to the next phase of his life—the phase that was much more appealing and important to him than the *present* moment.

After six months, John finally finished the house.

He went back to his boss, and told him, "I did what you asked. Now I am asking, one last time, for your blessing to retire."

His boss beamed. "Thank you, John! We just have one more thing."

John was beginning to get really upset because he thought they were going to ask him to build another house.

His boss reached into his desk and pulled out a small black box with a red ribbon tied around it. He handed the box to John. "We are so grateful for you. This gift is a token of our appreciation."

John pulled the ribbon and opened the box to discover a set of shiny new keys.

"The house is yours! You were the most important client we ever had!"

John's heart sank. Unbeknownst to him, he had been building his own house the whole time. If he had only known the house was for him, he would have cared so much more. He would have only used the finest materials, and he would have overseen every detail and given it his all like he had always done.

Now it was too late.

If I can be honest with you, one of my greatest challenges in life is remembering that I am *always* building my own house. I am an achiever. I love climbing the mountains and chasing the lions in my life. It is so easy to get caught up in those obsessions and forget that, with every little decision, I am building my own house.

The truth is, the only thing that is truly significant about today, or any other day, is who you become in the process.[1]

We are each building our own house, with every decision, big and small, every single day. My hope and prayer for each of us is that we build wisely.

---

1 If you want more detail about this concept, read, *Chop Wood Carry Water: How to Fall in Love With the Process of Becoming Great.*

CHAPTER 2

YOU CAN DO THIS

In 2003, I went to Vanderbilt on a partial soccer scholarship. We only had 2.1 scholarships for the coach to divvy up between the thirty-man roster as he saw fit. For three years, I was a struggling head case who got suspended from the team on five occasions. Everyone thought I was one of the best players on the team, but I couldn't translate my ability to high-level on-field performance. My stats were mediocre over those three years, and then the administration canceled our program when we came back from Christmas break during my junior year.

My dad grew up in a trailer park, and I now had the chance to graduate from a top 20 school. So with no one beating down my door to transfer and play for them, I decided to hang up my cleats and focus on school.

The following year, I went out for the club soccer team.

I had just booked a flight to Arizona for nationals when one of the captains called. He had been a walk-on on our varsity team for one year, and on the phone, he said, "Hey, man. I'm sorry, but the captains decided you aren't going to be on the roster. They outvoted me two to one. You should try and get a refund for your flight." Three months later, Joe Germanese, who had transferred to Duke when our program was cut, called me on my birthday and asked if I was interested in playing at Duke.

"I have a better question!" I blurted out. "Is the number one team in the country interested in a guy who had mediocre stats, who got kicked off the team five times, and who just got cut from the club team?!"

He told me he had vouched for me and said they had scholarship money available.

Five months later, I had a full ride to work on a master of arts in liberal studies. It wasn't all roses and butterflies though—when we played pickup games, my teammates always chose me dead last.

At that same time, I was taking a sports psychology class with Dr. Greg Dale, who told us he believed sports are over 70 percent mental. If that were the case, then why had no one taught us to train mentally?! I had done a lot of physical training, tons of technical training, but no one in twenty two years had taught me how to train mentally. If sports were over 70% mental, than a lot of people had failed me.

Under normal circumstances, I would have completely written this guy off, but I was desperate! *I was the last pick on the team,* so I decided to give his crazy ideas a shot. From the middle of the season on, I went from being the last pick, to finishing second in points to Mike Grella, our best player, who later opened his pro career with a hat trick for Leeds United. I became the Duke Student-Athlete of the Week and the ACC Player of the Week. Before getting to Duke, I had never scored a goal with my head but ended up scoring two goals with my head that season after learning how to use visualization.

I had a dramatic transformation, and then I started sharing these same tools with others and saw them have incredible results as well.

After Duke, I turned down scholarship offers to law school and moved across the country to live and serve at a homeless shelter in Echo Park, just outside downtown Los Angeles, California. I told the director of my program at Duke that instead of writing my master's thesis, I was going to create an organization that would change the world. It probably sounded crazy at the time. Matter of fact, *it was crazy,* but I knew in my gut it was what I needed to do. I knew that sharing the tools I had learned at Duke with the world would change millions of lives.

I lived and in the homeless shelter for seven months, and then I moved into the closet of a gym just south of LA to become a sports director for a local church and start my organization. I lived in the closet of the gym for nine months before my mom came out to stay with me. She saw the passion burning in my eyes and realized I was in this for the long haul. My father had passed away a couple of years before, which brought my mom and I even closer together, and she wanted to support my dream.

A few months later, we moved into an apartment in LA. During this time, I would go into Watts and South Central LA to train the athletes in one of the toughest areas in the country: the Imperial Courts housing projects. I taught those athletes sports, but more importantly, I was incorporating the mental training skills I had learned at Duke.

While in LA, I read and studied everything I could find on mental training and personal development. Most days I would read for ten to twelve hours. I would eventually create the brand, *Train to Be Clutch*, a hearts first approach to mental training, life skills, and leadership. We created the first mental training apps in the world for basketball, soccer, and golf. I eventually served as the director of mental training for UCLA Women's Basketball for seven years and have provided hundreds of workshops and keynotes around the world.

In the summer of 2015, IMG Academy was aggressively pursuing me to head up its mental conditioning and leadership program. Had I taken the position, they would have owned anything I created as their work product. This presented a challenge. I knew there was no go-to book in sport psychology, and I wanted to write it—and own it. Most of the people teaching sport psychology were simply regurgitating things they read in books and had never played at a high level or tested what they were talking about under the bright lights. While contemplating taking the position, I spent two months barely leaving my bed, furiously writing both the go-to book in sport psychology and my memoir. My roommates were very worried about me during this time, and my body atrophied quite a bit, as I was only out of bed for maybe thirty minutes each day.

Chop Wood Carry Water went on to blow my greatest expectations out of the water. It is self-published and routinely outsells some of the biggest names in the entire writing world. It is used all over the world by everyone from six-year-olds to professional athletes in every sport to finance, law, real estate, and sales professionals to specialists in things I don't even understand (I'm looking at you, forensic engineering). Since then, I've continued to write more books to address the issues I saw while in the trenches with people in sports, business, and education.

You could make an argument that it was luck that turned my soccer career around at Duke, but fifteen years later it's happened again with my golf, proving that mind-blowing transformation is possible with hard, smart work. I truly hope you can use the inspiration from my story, the exercises in this book, and the mindset I am teaching to take your game to the next level.

Don't worry about where you are currently at with golf.

Maybe you just started playing golf during the pandemic. Maybe you are on the PGA Tour. It doesn't matter where you currently are. The ideas and exercises in this book can help you get better and build your game. Let's just focus on getting better.

The beauty of what has transpired over the past fifteen years is that when I played soccer at Duke, I only had two months to experiment and use these tools. It wasn't until my first club championship in 2021 that I was able to live out the ideas I had been training myself and others with for over a decade.

I'm not special. Sometimes I always wondered deep down if I was special and just got lucky while playing soccer at Duke. After seeing how I was able to play in our club championship at San Diego Country Club in 2021, I realized anyone can see the benefits of this type of training.

I'm not special.

You can do this.

Talent isn't as important as the work and dedication necessary to become competent.
—Jack Nicklaus

CHAPTER 3

THE STRUGGLE

MY DAD GREW up in a trailer park where they literally had to duct tape their trailer to hold it together. My grandfather walked out on the family when my dad was still in diapers, and I only met him once. He was badly addicted to alcohol, and his "home" was one of the saddest things I had ever seen.

When I was six years old, I vividly remeber dreaming about getting a Happy Meal from McDonald's. On a great day, my and I would split a thirty-nine-cent cheeseburger and an ice cream cone. My mom loved sports and taught my brothers and I how to play all the sports that didn't require much money to play.

My dad had worked very hard to overcome his circumstances and somehow went from selling drugs as a kid to becoming an eye surgeon. He was quite stubborn, and after being rejected by the ophthalmology residency he wanted for six years, they finally let him in after they realized he was never going to give up.

During my dad's medical residency, we spent three years in Chicago and three in Detroit. After his Ophthalmology Fellowship Training in Akron, Ohio, my parents moved us back to Oklahoma where they had grown up.

My dad embodied the American dream.

We got a small house two blocks from where he was starting his eye practice. The day we got the keys, my dad threw my fully clothed brothers and me into our very own pool. I was almost nine years old, and it was one of the best days of my childhood.

The following summer, our American dream turned into an American nightmare. My baby brother and best friend was two and a half years old. He was a little freak athlete who was always getting into trouble. One afternoon, my mom and I were in the living room trying to organize a bookshelf, when my mom realized we couldn't hear Jordan. She started calling for him and looking all around the house.

Her voice became more and more frantic, until it turned into a guttural scream. It was as if her voice was the gunshot at a track meet. I've always had a gift for understanding things at levels I can't easily explain, and even at nine years old, I knew instantly that my baby brother was in the pool. I bolted for the back door and within seconds was diving into the pool to get him out. He was lifeless at the bottom when I got to him.

I wrote about this story and what transpired afterward in my memoir, *Hustle*, but the short version is that my brother's death became the defining moment of my youth.

I became angry in ways I couldn't even begin to describe. On top of that, it would be two decades later before I would learn that I am on the autism spectrum. Put together, the trauma of losing my brother and being completely misunderstood put a freight-ship-sized chip on my shoulder.

Etched into my mind is my middle brother, Jonathan, yelling at me, "Why can't you just be normal?" My solace came from immersing myself in sports, especially training. From a very young age, I would throw myself into training. It's why my first love was basketball. I could train on my own and lose myself with just a ball—I didn't even need a hoop. Later in life, I would find the same solace in training with golf.

Eventually I realized not only was training therapeutic for me, it was also a cheat code for getting ahead in sports. However, most of my childhood was lived in my younger brother's shadow. He was a natural at almost every sport he tried. He did a rainbow in a soccer game at six years old. His coach spit out his coffee and blurted out, "That little shit just did a rainbow!" Not only had he pulled off an amazing move for any soccer player, he did it in a game to get around a player. He got his first hole in one at thirteen years old after only playing a few rounds of golf.

As you can probably imagine, it always felt like I never quite measured up as a kid. I was a great athlete by all objective measures, but I was awkward, both playing sports and with people. Senior year, I had a knee injury the doctors couldn't figure out, and I had to sit out the entire high school season. The day after every game, people would pass me in the halls and say "Great game!" confusing me with my brother, who was a freshman, and led the team in scoring. We lived in Oklahoma at the time, which only added to my inferiority complex. Who knew how we stacked up to others around the country?

My self-doubt got worse when I tried out for the best club soccer team in the city. Even though I was good enough to make the team, the captains voted three to one to pass on me. They hated playing against me and thought they would hate playing *with* me.

That year I single-handedly beat them on my terrible team, so they reluctantly let me join the following year. My self-doubt still reigned, however. People told me, "You aren't going to get playing time for Tulsa Nationals," and although I proved them wrong by leading Tulsa Nationals to back-to-back state titles and a regional championship, a nagging voice permanently echoed in my head. *You don't belong. You're a weirdo.* And most destructive of all: *They only put up with you because you're good.*

Most of my life experiences confirmed that track in my mind. My scholarships to play soccer at Vanderbilt and Duke were based solely on athletic ability, with both schools using "special slots" because I was so far off from their academic standards.

I vividly remember scoring a goal during a scrimmage freshmen year and my coach yelling out, "Yes! That's why I brought you here, that goofy shit!" It was quite jarring. Playing soccer before everyone had high-quality video recording on their phone, I didn't really know how awkward I was when I played. I was good at getting the job done, but apparently I did it by doing "goofy shit."

Having high hand-eye coordination and athleticism with no formal golf coaching turned out to be quite the liability on the golf course. Over years of only playing every couple of months, I manipulated the club and my stance more and more, creating many bad habits I would have to overcome for the rest of my golf life.

Golf is a game of opposites. I didn't learn that until I started working with Sam Cyr, so for years, I twisted myself further and further into a pretzel to hit the ball using only my athleticism. In no time, bad habits became terrible habits.

Reverse every natural instinct and do the opposite of what you are inclined to do, and you will probably come very close to having a perfect golf swing.
—Ben Hogan

The first time it happened, I wasn't quite sure what it was. The ball shot dead right off my club, and I don't mean a slice. I mean it shot out three feet off the ground and dead right. I dropped another ball and swung again. Same thing.

The dreaded hosel shanks had crept in. I didn't know why it was happening, and the harder I tried to fix it, the worse it got. I battled the hosels for a year and a half. It got so bad by the end that I was putting from 150 yards and in. If I couldn't hit a hybrid or a driver, then I was using a putter.

It was traumatizing. It still is. It is like Voldemort, I hate when I even hear someone say the word "shanks". Sometimes it feels like just mentioning them will summon them from the depths of hell.

However, I could still find a way to break 90 with a lot of five-foot gimmes, but it was embarrassing. Can you imagine getting paired with a guy who is putting 150 yards from the hole? To this day, there is little I fear in sports more than the dreaded shanks.

It was so embarrasing during that time, and it lasted for over a year and a half. I loved the game, but I didn't know if I would ever get over the dreaded hosel rockets.

CHAPTER 4

TIGER WOODS AT TORREY PINES

AFTER PLAYING LACROSSE throughout college, Jenn Tapscott moved to San Diego. She and I got to Vanderbilt at the same time and to this day we call each other "brother" and "sister" because of how close we are and how similar we look. In the summer of 2008, I decided I would visit her, and by sheer happenstance, the US Open was being held nearby at Torrey Pines Golf Course. I didn't think I could afford a ticket, but I decided to check anyway. Shockingly, I was able to secure a ticket for the final round for ninety dollars. Not in my wildest imagination could I have conceived what I would witness that day. One hundred thirty yards from the green on the eighteenth hole, I watched in awe as my sports hero, Tiger Woods, made one of his most historic and clutch putts to force a playoff with Rocco Mediate. He would go on to win what looked like for almost a decade, his final major.

People often ask me what brought me to San Diego, and they are usually a little confused when I tell them, "Torrey Pines Golf Course." City residents can walk the two courses for less than fifty dollars at twilight, and for a kid who knew nothing about junior memberships at country clubs, this seemed like the best deal in the world.

Thirteen years after watching Tiger make that iconic putt, I'm lying one from the middle of the fairway on that same hole with only 180 yards to the hole. I'm one over par. With an eagle, I shoot under par.[2]

It had felt like a special day when I got to the first tee box. The wind is almost always in your face at Torrey Pines, and it seemed to be blowing about 12 miles per hour that day. I hadn't hit balls and wasn't warmed up,

---

2 I was playing from the black tees. Golfers at Torrey Pines need written permission to play the tournament tees, even professional golfers.

but for some reason everything felt different that morning. I had been in the gym for many months doing a lot of speed work. Something had clicked, and I had added considerable distance. I looked at the right bunker and said to myself, "You can cover the left side with a draw." I piped it over the corner, and I felt many limiting beliefs shatter in my mind. I typically had over two hundred yards in, but when I got to my ball I only had 170 yards left to a back pin.

Seventeen tee shots later, I've got a great chance to shoot under par on a US Open course, albeit not in US Open conditions or from the tournament tees.

The pin was tucked front-right, just over the water—almost exactly where Tiger made his putt. Typically, I'm a very conservative golfer, but I decided this could be a once-in-a-lifetime opportunity. I pull my five wood and am going to try and slice one in there close. I would have preferred it be 190 yards for this shot. I don't hit my irons high or with a ton of spin, so a five iron, my 180-yard club, would have little chance of getting close.

I hit a smooth slice, and it is tracking right at the pin. The only thing I am worried about is if I took too much off it.

Sure enough, it hits the bank and crawls up a few feet before trickling back and then careening into the water. Had it flown another two yards, I would have had a putt inside ten feet to shoot one under.

I settled for a bogey and a 74. While I was sad I didn't pull it off a sub-par round, I left with a whole new perspective on the possibilities of my golf game.

The old hustler, Mike Defay, played with me that day. At seventy-three years old, Mike doesn't have the power he once had, but his short game is infamous. He still shoots in the 70s a few times a year. He was my first partner when I played in a big-money game at San Diego Country Club. I remember thinking, *Oh no! I've got this guy as my partner! He looks like he is going to keel over dead at any moment!*

It only took a few holes for me to realize that, between the two of us, I was the weak link. I had never played in a game where you had to putt everything outside of an actual foot. (When most amateur golfers say a putt is a foot, it's three feet, and when they say three feet, it's actually five to seven feet from the hole.)

Mike might not hit it far, but he is a wizard on the greens at our club. I had played probably three hundred rounds of golf with him at our club and many other clubs around the country. He had a front-row seat to my transformation. He had watched me go from a terrible putter to one of the best in our group. But it was after that day at Torrey he told people, "Joshua is virtually unbeatable. The length he has added in such a short amount of time is unbelievable."

People don't understand that when I was growing up, I was never the most talented and I was not the biggest. I was never the fastest. I certainly was never the strongest. The only thing I had was my work ethic, and that's what has gotten me this far.
—Tiger Woods

CHAPTER 5

"YOU GOTTA MEET SAM!"

GOLF WAS, AND still predominantly is, a rich man's game. The first time I ever touched a club was when I was thirteen years old, and my mom had sent my younger brother and I to a twenty-five-dollar camp at—*Little Links* in Broken Arrow, Oklahoma. Once my father became an eye surgeon, things were looking up for us financially, but green fees and country club initiations still left golf far out of reach.

I loved golf, but it would be a long time before I could afford to play consistently. One of the biggest challenges for people who didn't grow up in a country club is that we tend to teach ourselves how to play. We didn't have a solid foundation ingrained in us when our brains and motor skills were most malleable and ready for it. This leads us to try to figure it out as we play and lifelong bad habits that are hard to break. Without building a solid foundation, it becomes very hard to ever get good. Weekend golfers love to share the latest "tips" they heard from a good player or a coach. In the end, there's a lot of "the blind leading the blind."

Without a teaching expert watching you and showing you how to improve your unique swing, you're likely to end up with even more bad habits. Then the "tips" get you so messed up, you finally book a one-off lesson.

Working with a coach on the range or in a hitting bay can feel good. But it's a fleeting feeling. Going out after that is a lot like trying to remember how to do algebra at home after learning it that morning in class. Your old bad habits sneak back into your swing because you haven't spent enough time ingraining the right mechanics. It's incredibly hard to build a solid swing that can hold up under pressure with just a few lessons here and there, especially if you're not sticking to one coach or method. This is one of the reasons why so many people end up with mismatched swings and consequently look like a child who dressed themselves in the dark.

When I post my swing on social media, swing coaches always want to give me tips. I respectfully tell them, "I have one coach, and I only listen to him."

In 2014, I gave a keynote at the WGCA convention, which most of the women's college golf coaches from all over the country attend. This generated a lot of interest in our brand, and I started working with a lot of those golf programs. For the first time in my life, I had access to better golf than I had ever been able to afford. Greg Towne is the women's golf coach at Indiana State University, and he played professionally all over the world for twenty-five years. He came to one of our Train to Be Clutch retreats and started fixing my swing and getting me over the hosel rockets. He and I are great friends to this day, and he was my first real coach.

The day after I moved to San Diego in 2016, I went to a golf outing a local church was hosting. After telling one of the leaders some of the things I'd done in the sports world, he said, "You've got to meet Sam!"

At the time, Samuel Cyr had been playing on the *Asian Tour* for about five years and had been playing professionally for twelve after winning two individual national championships at Point Loma University. I signed a copy of *Chop Wood Carry Water* and *Pound the Stone* for him in the parking lot that day, and we exchanged numbers. Over the next few months, we played a few times when he came back from Asia, but then he got sick.

It wasn't the first time it had happened over there, and he decided to slow down his Asia schedule so he could get healthy. We started playing together three or four times a week. I'd moved to San Diego so I could retire and play golf, which allowed me to play with him almost anytime. We became fast friends.

For the first ten to fifteen rounds we played together, I never saw him miss a shot, not even slightly. Every round he would shoot 63 to 66 as casually as I tap in a three-inch putt. It was mind-blowing to watch him play, and I realized very quickly that his golf IQ was freakishly high. He didn't just go out and hit the ball, he was thinking about and calculating a hundred different things before every shot. Sam is naturally a giving human and often puts the needs of others ahead of his own, so he can't help but teach every time he is playing with people. Often he would run through his thought process aloud, providing me with a unique opportunity to learn from a savant.

Over time, I started to notice the benefits of these little nuggets of golf wisdom. It took a few years to fully understand how amazing of a teacher he is because we usually played by ourselves; my autism made me very bristly when he would bring people I didn't know to play with us. As I got better, though—especially when I would bring my friends to play with him—I started to realize that Sam is easily one of the best teachers in the world.

One of my best friends started playing recently and is taking lessons from Sam. He calls Sam "The Phil Jackson of golf coaching." Sam is very conservative in life and on the golf course, so as a natural byproduct of playing close to five hundred rounds with him and caddying for him in some of his professional events, my golf game has started to emulate his. I have become so conservative on the golf course my close friends have a hard time believing that is how I play.

Typically, how a person plays golf is an extension and reflection of their personality. If they have anger problems, that will come out. If they are aggressive, they will never lay up. If they are a tentative person, they play tentative golf, and so forth.

As someone who passed on scholarships to law school, didn't write his master's thesis at Duke, lived in a homeless shelter for seven months and the closet of a gym for nine months, loves jumping off waterfalls, and does crazy stuff for his age and skill level on a snowboard, the way I play golf doesn't make much sense. I have become an incredibly conservative golfer.

One of my friends at San Diego Country Club has been scratch most of his life and won a lot of big amateur tournaments in his twenties and thirties. He says, "Anytime Joshua has a wedge in his hand, I expect it's going in." Yet most of the time I will putt or hit a safer bump-and-run shot in a big match because the numbers say it's the smarter play. Why am I like this? *Sam Cyr.*

Whether you want it to happen, whether you believe it or not, the people you choose to play with are going to have a big impact on the type of player you become.

I was caddying for a friend the other day and noticed a few alarming tendencies in the way he plays. On the way home, I told him that the people he plays with and admires had rubbed off on him and encouraged some really bad habits. His case is particularly difficult because one of the friends he plays golf with is one of the best players in the world. However, my friend is not, and things the tour pro can get away with have hurt his game.

For better or worse, we become more like the people we play with. You want to play with people who look at every tough situation golf throws at them as an opportunity for special.

I smile at obstacles.
—Tiger Woods

Golf lessons can be very expensive, but I always tell people, *"Cheap is always more expensive in the long run."*

Growing up the way I did, the only thing we had heard about country clubs is that they were outrageously expensive, so I never thought I could afford to join one. I was also on a mission to play the top one hundred public courses in America, which I considered another disincentive to becoming a member.

But one day, Sam invited me to play at San Diego Country Club. After the round, the membership director gave me information, and I realized with how much I played that I would actually save money by joining.

At the time, it was $6,500 to join and $550 a month for a junior membership (for those under forty years old). I could even prorate the $6,500 into my monthly bill, so all I needed to pay up front was $1,500.

Soon after joining the club, I met three guys who would change my life in golf: Akash "Scottie" Patel, Brent Lawrence, and Darryl Miller. These guys are salt-of-the-earth people and some of the best adult amateurs in SoCal. Scottie is the GOAT. He's won almost every invitational in the region and has earned so much influence and goodwill that we call him the mayor of SoCal golf. He's a two-time club champ at San Diego Country Club and has a swing that's as smooth as butter. He also has ice in his veins—the bigger the moment, the better he is. I've had the privilege of working with some of the top performers in the world in a variety of different sports, and there's only one other person that has that type of ice in their veins like him.

Scottie and Brent are best friends and played almost every single day at 11:00 a.m.

I realized very quickly that they liked playing for big money, at least it felt like big money to me. I had never gambled for more than twenty dollars, but they routinely were playing for hundreds or thousands of dollars. It would be a couple of years before I realized no one wins or loses very much in the end. The money just changes hands back and forth throughout the year.

I just knew that those were the guys I wanted to play with, so if high-stakes gambling was what it took to get in their circle, then I was happy to pay for the access.

I looked up to and admired each of them in different ways, but none like Scottie. It was in the way Scottie interacted with people and how he would play with everyone—from up-and-coming juniors, to the old guys, to guys who weren't very good. Everyone loved Scottie, and everyone loved when he played with them. Scottie and I couldn't have more different personalities on and off the golf course, but I realized very early on that I wanted to emulate his game and the way he treated people.

Being the fierce competitor that I am, as well as someone who has never tried to fit in, the social dynamics of the country club were a big learning curve for me. I burned a lot of bridges and rubbed a lot of people the wrong way in my first couple years. Thankfully, though, the more time I spent around Scottie, Brent, and Darryl, the more I became like them.

Two years before winning the club championship, Scottie said something to me and one of my best golf friends, Casey Young, that I couldn't even process at the time. It seemed so unattainable and detached from any sense of reality. He said, "You two are going to be the next me and Brent. It will be your responsibility to carry on the tradition and make this club better."

Uh, what?

I couldn't really wrap my head around what he was saying. Sure, CY and I were good players, but we were nothing compared to Brent and Scottie. Their handicaps would get down to around +3 every summer and were legends who routinely won all the biggest partner tournaments in SoCal.

Casey and I, however, had never really sniffed being scratch, and when we would get down to our lowest handicaps from the men's tees, for him a 2 and me a 3, we had an impossible time competing at those numbers.

However, when the sad day came that Scottie and Brent left the club in April of 2021, I remembered what Scottie had said, and I took it very seriously. It was our responsibility, and I didn't want to let my golf mentor down. I started working hard on my game and shifted my focus from gambling golf to becoming a better ambassador for the club like Scottie had always been.

Wilshire Country Club hosts, *The Macbeth*, an invitational that is nearly impossible to get into. After hearing about it for a couple years, I begged Scottie to make a phone call to get me and Casey in. Fifteen minutes after the call Scottie made and said "wouldn't do anything," we got an email that we were in.

The first year we played in it, I sucked. My handicap was a 6 for the tournament, and I couldn't come close to playing to it. I played, at best, like a 12 and knew I had a lot of work to do in order to compete at a higher level. I realized tournament golf is a very different animal than gambling with your buddies.

Due to the global pandemic, for the first time in one hundred years the tournament didn't take place in 2020, so I wanted to make sure I was ready for 2021.

Scottie and Brent left the club about five months before *The Macbeth*. That was when I started working out four or five days a week and did speed work to add distance to my driver. Because I developed a hernia earlier in the year, I couldn't go crazy in the gym. Here is what my gym routine looked like almost every morning Monday to Friday:

- Stairmaster level 13–17 for 4 minutes (2 sets)
- Perfect pushups, 10–15 reps (8–10 sets)
- Dumbbell curls and shoulder press (3 sets)
- TRX 3 suspension trainer back pulls (3 sets)
- Perfect pushups, 10–15 reps (8–10 sets)
- Mach 3 SpeedBomber, 15 swings (3 sets)
- Plank (3 sets)
- Medicine ball side-to-side abs (3 sets)

I stopped drinking alcohol when I played and focused on putting and chipping every week. When *The Macbeth* rolled around, I felt pretty good about my game. I had just gotten down to a zero index, and it was time to see how it held up under pressure.

My favorite clubs are the blacked-out Miura TC-201s, but they are forged clubs with a very small head. Right before I left for *The Macbeth*, I went to storage and pulled out an older set of mine with a more forgiving forged head, the Mizuno JPX 919s.

The first two days are best ball with your partner, and I wasn't thrilled with my performance. The final day is aggregate. Each partner had to play out their ball until it was in the hole, and every shot counted. We started on hole 10, which is a tricky par 3 with a skinny, odd-shaped green that can play anywhere from 105 to 175 yards.

I hit it twenty feet below the pin, and my partner hit the front right bunker. He ended up digging a hole in the bunker like he was looking for gold, and on his fourth attempt, he bladed the ball into the lip, and it somehow crawled over the lip and out. He had had a rough first two days, and I was keeled over, almost crying with laughter. I couldn't help it. If there was any pressure on our performance, he eliminated most of it by starting off with a quadruple bogey. After regaining my composure, I hit my putt. It burned the edge and needed just one more rotation to have gone in. It came to rest three inches past the hole. I tapped it in for par. The next hole was a beautiful and tight par 4 guarded by bunkers and a creek in front of the green. I hit a good drive, then hit my pitching wedge just a bit long on my approach. I was facing a slippery twenty-foot putt with about four feet of break. I hit another great putt and left it dead in the heart, just one foot short.

I tapped it in for par. The next hole is a cool par 4—gorgeous homes lining the right side and a doglegging fairway with a creek snaking down the left. After a good drive, I had a twenty-five-foot birdie putt from below the hole. Once again, I left it dead in the heart, hanging on the edge. I was both frustrated that I could be three under and ecstatic about how well I was hitting it. I tried to remind myself that they would eventually start falling.

Next hole: a par 3 with two different greens. There was a tiny green to the left that could be used for a delicate 80-yard shot, but that day they had the course set for the right green, which was closer to 185 yards. I hit a great tee ball and gave myself another twenty-foot putt below the hole.

Right before hitting the putt, I told myself to make sure I got this one to the hole. Had it not hit the hole, I would have had a lengthy come back for par. Thankfully, it hit the back of the cup, putting me at one under par.

The next hole was a crazy par 5. The fairway is about 200 feet higher on the right side than the left, with everything funneling to the same large creek from the earlier hole and rough on the left. I manage to navigate it with a good drive and five wood. In the end, I had a six-foot birdie putt, but it was a slick one with two cups of break. I paused and breathed deeply, then hit a perfect putt. Two under par.

The next hole was a 306-yard par 4 with the driving range fence down the left side and homes all along the right side. There is a perfectly placed death bunker right in the middle of the fairway 230 to 250 yards out. If I hit short of the bunker, I would have around 135 yards for my approach to a very small and slopey green. I decided to hit driver, and my tee ball landed just short of pin high, 35 yards to the left of the green.

The problem was that I now had an extremely difficult chip to the tiniest part of the green with a landing area maybe the size of a small pool table. The greens were rolling around 13, and this would be the first of five pins on the edges of turtle-shaped greens. I hit one of the best shots of my life but left myself with a 2.5-foot downhill putt. If I did more than tap the putt and missed the hole, the ball would roll off the green and put me 30 feet away from the hole.

I got nervous and went quickly. Normally I had my partner plumb my putts, but this time, I just stepped up and tapped it. I tried to play it inside-right but started it closer to right-center. It lipped out. Thankfully, my par putt was a tap in from a foot, and it didn't roll off the edge of the green, but I was shook. I hit a terrible tee shot on the next hole and ended up making my first bogey.

The rest of the day I putted very tentatively. Instead of trying to make putts, I was trying to putt everything inside of a foot to avoid missing a two-footer again. Seven different times I would have made putts had they just had one or two more rotations of speed.

Overall, I hit it incredibly well and always put myself in great positions—until the last hole. I bailed out short-right and left myself the hardest putt of the day—at least 50 feet from the hole and around 10 feet of break, which ran away at the end. I came up 8 feet short, which left me with a slick putt to shoot one under.

After looking at it from all the angles, I took a deep breath and put a good stroke on it. It looked like it was going to hang out-right, and then at the very last moment, it broke just enough to catch the edge and toilet-bowl into the hole. The two guys we played with were members at Wilshire Country Club and were incredibly impressed with how I had played. I was excited but also frustrated because I knew if I had made the short one on hole 6, I probably would have gone on to shoot the round of my life at four to six under par.

It wasn't until writing this book I realized all the mental mistakes I made during that round. Had I been practicing what I teach tour pros, I would have been doing my What Went Well" journaling on my pin sheet.[3] I would have been directing my focus to all the great putts and drives that I was hitting instead of allowing my focus to be on the one short putt that I missed. I allowed one mistake to compound into more mistakes instead of riding the momentum of my hot putter.

This is one of the main reasons I teach my clients to carry a performance cue card with them as they play. It is very easy to get derailed by our experiences in the moment, and we need constant reminders of all the little things that make a big difference.

We had teed off in the morning, and it wasn't until later that evening that I realized just how special my round was. I kept checking every ten minutes as the scores came in until the very last one had posted. In a field of two hundred players, including fifteen club champs like Tony Behrstock, the seventeen-time club champ at Hillcrest in Los Angeles, I

---

3 Visit https://www.t2bc.com/hack for a printable What Went Well pin sheet journal, performance cue card, and good reminders.

had tied for low gross with five other guys. Tony shot 79. The club champ from Wilshire shot 79.

I shot 70.

I couldn't believe it. The glass ceiling in my mind shattered. I realized that when I was on, I could compete with some of the best around. My A-game had tied low gross. I realized at that moment that all of my training with Sam was starting to shine through.[4] The games I normally played didn't favor consistency; our bets at the club generally favored the last five holes, which I didn't always play well on. But in a stroke-play event where every shot matters, the consistent and conservative way Sam had taught me to play was able to shine.

Remember: the people who will have the greatest influence on who you become are the people you spend the most time with and the people you admire the most.

All I ever wanted to do was play competitive golf against the best players in the world.
—Jack Nicklaus

---

4 I highly suggest booking a consultation call with Sam (samcyrgolf@gmail.com) to see if working with him is a good fit for your game.

CHAPTER 6

ALL HARD WORK IS NOT EQUAL

IF YOU FALL in love with the process, you will <u>eventually</u> love what the process produces. Most of what we call luck and talent is simply a willingness to put in a disgusting amount of effort into honing one's craft.

The problem with golf, though, is that there are so many different areas you can work on. *What* you work on and *how* you work make a massive impact on the results of your hard work. *Not all hard work is equal.*

If you spend seven hours a day on the driving range, don't be surprised if you lose to a person who only spends a couple of hours a day *doing hard, focused, deliberate practice.* [5] Research has shown that focused bursts of practice are more important than long, unfocused, and sloppy practice. Most people know that the driving range is nothing like the course, but rarely does that translate into how they practice.

Your swing speed is typically lower on the range, your heart rate is lower on the range, you don't have hazards on the range, and you don't have to worry about short-siding yourself on the range. Swing speed is slower on the range because our focus is on hitting the ball solid, whereas on the course, we are trying to hit the ball a very specific distance and tend to increase club speed to try and get the ball to go that distance.

One of the big issues with range time is that most people use the range for block practice. Block practice is doing the same thing over and over again. In golf, this means hitting with the same club again and again. Research has shown that block practice only increases retention in the

---

5 For more on the subject of Deliberate Practice, read *The Talent Code*, by Daniel Coyle.

short term—that same day. This is why so many coaches and players fall in love with it. They can see immediate results, and it makes them *feel* better.

This short-term quality of block practice, however, is also what makes it wickedly deceptive. It covers up our flaws and weaknesses, which leads to more frustration on the course—which then leads to going back to the range to "work things out." The cycle repeats itself over and over.

The day after block practice, the improvement we saw on the range regresses, and we get frustrated because we wonder why all our hard work isn't paying off. Eventually it feels pointless, and honestly, it kind of is. It is the wrong kind of hard work.

Have you ever noticed that when you drop another ball and hit a second one out on the course, Player B is a lot better?

It's not an accident. Player B has a million more bits of information than Player A had.

Now let's play this out when you are on the range practicing and only change clubs every ten to fifteen shots. How much more information do Players C, D, E, F, G, H, I, J, K, L, M, N, O, and P have?

The answer: *tens of millions.* It is like cheating and those players don't get to play. Only Player A gets to play out on the course, and Player A gets virtually no reps with block practice on the range.

The best way to practice is called "random practice." With random practice you never hit the same shot or use the same club twice in a row. This topic has been one of the three main causes of arguments I have had with players and coaches over the years. People *love* block practice. They *hate* random practice. Random practice is messy, and you don't see immediate results like you do with block practice.

What are the benefits of random practice? Long-term retention. The day after random practice, more of what you worked on actually sticks with you. When the effects of block practice have worn off, the slow growth of random practice builds.

The only time block practice trumps random practice is the day of big events. That is where the short-term effects of block practice are what we want.

Day of competition: Use Block practice

Every other day: Use Random practice

If you insist on using block practice to build a new skill, then I would refer to how Ben Pellacani teaches his players. Ben is an excellent golf coach who has incorporated much of our curriculum into his teaching for many years:

Block practice has its place, like when you are first learning a new skill, drill, or making a change in your golf swing. Where people get off track is understanding the point of the practice stations or drills. They are not medicine—such as, do them five hundred times, and you are cured. They are opportunities to learn. The early stages (first five to twenty balls) of a new skill, Players A through Z are fine to get the base skill ingrained. After this early phase, when a player is starting to feel comfortable in the new skill, that player should quickly add variety and situational shots into their drill or station. For example, hit four balls in your station, hitting the first one your stock yardage, the second one high, the third one low, and the fourth one five yards less than your stock yardage. Then step outside your station and grab a different club, hitting one draw, one fade, and one five yards shorter than normal. Randomized practice in the same drill allows a player to learn and grow and be able to handle the one-off situation that is the game of golf while also building their technique.

Other ways to randomize a station or drill are with tempo or yardages. Hit three balls in your drill with a full swing at 30 percent, 70 percent, then 105 percent. If you have a launch monitor, use a random number generator setting it between your max yardage for that club and twenty-five yards less. Then try to hit a random yardage using the launch monitor as feedback.

Personally, I would prefer that all of your practice be random. Before I learned about the benefits of random practice, I would go out and hit buckets and buckets of balls. It was very frustrating to feel as though I was working hard but not seeing my range sessions translate to the course. When I first started working with Greg Towne, no matter the skill we were trying to build, I would change clubs on every swing. The following summer after putting from 150 yards and in, I shot a 69. Now, this wasn't in a tournament or even while gambling. But I saw the effects of committing to random practice.

The past two years, I spent very little time at the range practicing because I prefer to practice by playing. However, when I do practice at the range, I change clubs after every swing. Forty-five minutes is the most time I spend hitting balls at the range outside of warming up for a round, and I might do this once every two months. When I do traditional practice, it is on my putting mat at home or the putting green and chipping area at our club.

When I worked with Laura Diaz from the LPGA Tour, I encouraged her to practice just like she played:

Hit a driver to a target, then pick a pin in the distance, and hit to that pin.

- If the green was hit with the approach, then walk over to the putting green and put out from the approximate distance of the approach shot.
- Repeat this process again and again, playing different types of holes in your imagination.

This is much easier at some facilities than others. At my club, it is a bit of a walk from the putting green to the range and same with the chipping area. I do not move from one to the other and simply incorporate random practice at each of the areas.

When I was the director of mental training for UCLA Women's Basketball, I had the coaches implement something similar for free throws. The players needed to make a certain amount of free throws before they were done for the day, so I took inspiration from a real-game situation. Rather than stand and shoot until all the free throws were made, each player was only allowed three shots in a row since that is the most a player can earn in a row without a lane violation. We would also distract them with noises and such to try and shake them up. Tiger Wood's father trained him in a similar manner when he was young. He would do all sorts of things to bother Tiger while he was training and playing.

It's sad, but working hard in golf doesn't mean it's going to pay off in the ways you want. In the most frustrating and ironic twist, it can actually make you worse, because the harder you work, the higher your expectations. The higher your expectations, the worse you actually perform. Have you ever heard the saying, "Beware of the ailing golfer"? An injured or sick golfer is dangerous because they have inadvertently surrendered the outcome and lowered their expectations. Therefore, their training and skills can more easily shine through.

When you work hard in ways that don't translate well to competition, it raises your expectations without raising your actual competition skill.

You start to think that how your Player B-Z hit the ball is how your Player A should hit the ball under duress in competition. Those increased expectations lead to extreme frustration and burnout because all that hard work feels like a waste of time. And again, I argue it *is* a waste of time. If you have been stuck in this cycle, it's time to work hard *and* smart.

All hard work is not equal.

Raising the expectations in your head is terrible. Fake training on the range and in soft settings raises your expectations.

Raising the beliefs of your heart is great. The toughest training—deep inner work—and competing against the best raises the beliefs of our hearts. We are always being subconsciously pulled in the direction of the deepest beliefs of our hearts. Deep down we know whether we have been forged in the fire or have been wasting time with soft drills and soft competition.

Remember: *block practice might make you feel better, but random practice actually helps you get better.*

CHAPTER 7

STATE-BASED LEARNING

Another big mistake that golfers make is listening to music when they train. Unless you can listen to music when you compete, I highly suggest not listening to music when you train.

Here is the rule: If you can listen to music during competition, then you should train with trigger songs. Create a highlight reel of you playing close to your best and put it to music—a song you love—and then watch and listen to it often. That song will become a trigger song and instantly put you in a more powerful state of mind when you hear it.

The problem with golf is that most of the time you cannot listen to music while competing.

Research has shown that *state-based learning* is a real thing, meaning whatever state you are in when you learn something, then that state is the state you need to be in to execute the skill again. Researchers got rats drunk and then taught them how to navigate a maze. When the rats would sober up, they would not remember how to navigate the maze. When they got them drunk again, the rats immediately remembered how to navigate the maze without being retaught.

This applies to everything. I've noticed that when I play in sweats out at public courses, I struggle more with my game. I'm in a different state when I am in sweats than when I am in country club attire. I always putt in my house with my shoes on for the same reason. It's different putting barefoot than it is in shoes. *Slight differences matter when added up and compounded over time.*[6]

---

6 For more on this, read *The Slight Edge* by Jeff Olson.

Another way this plays out is with heart rate. Whether you have felt it or measured it, your heart rate is significantly higher when competing than when on the range or out playing with your friends. The higher your heart rate, the harder it is to execute simple tasks. If you play golf at a high level, it is probably worth wearing something that measures your heart rate during competition to have a better understanding of where you need to get your heart rate during training.

One thing you can do to get your heart rate up during training is to jog to the ball in between your shots. To do this you need a pushcart or someone driving the cart with your clubs. I would not suggest doing this while carrying your bag. Our clients that play at very high levels have told us this exercise replicates what it feels like to hit shots under big-tournament pressure. Another way of getting your heart rate up is with pushups, burpees, or jumping jacks before shots. Greg Towne also has his team do wall sits in between reps to implement this type of heart rate training during their indoor winter training.[7]

The idea is to make our training more challenging than competition. *I want my training to be so tough that everything slows down for me in competition.*

Lastly, I always told my golf clients to train as if every shot is to win the US Open, then play in tournaments as if they are out having fun with their friends. Most people do the opposite, and not surprisingly, they play their best golf out with their friends. In our club championship, I could tell how nervous every one of my competitors was. I got to play with the joy and freedom that came from having trained hard, trained well, and surrendered the outcome.

One guy who was playing in the quarterfinals of our club championship played the best round of his year and holed out for birdie from the bunker on the eighteenth hole. He then walked up and conceded the match to his opponent. He had a trip planned for the next weekend and knew he

---

7 Check with your doctor before experimenting with any of these activities to make sure you are healthy enough for them.

couldn't play. In my opinion, it was that freedom that allowed more of his potential to shine through.

Golf is hard enough. Let's not make it harder than it has to be. Train in ways that allow your potential to come out when and where you really want it to.

Success depends almost entirely on how effectively you learn to manage the game's two ultimate adversaries: the course and yourself.
—Jack Nicklaus

CHAPTER 8

COMFORTABLE WITH UNCOMFORTABILITY

IN THE FALL of 2019, my good friend Jim Murphy invited me to Norway for cold-water training with *Inner Mountain Expeditions*. I politely declined. I was already planning to be in Iceland around that time for a photography trip, and while it wouldn't interfere, it didn't sound like something I wanted to do. I already knew the benefits of ice baths because they were the only thing that kept me on the soccer field at Vanderbilt and Duke.

Nevertheless, Jim insisted. I kept telling him no, but every couple of days, he would call me with an update. The most annoying part was that he was going for free, but I was going to have to pay full freight.

A couple weeks later, I was speaking in Florida and met up with one of my favorite people. Robyn and I met her freshmen year when she was playing golf at Indiana State for Greg Towne, and as we caught up over breakfast, she peppered me with great questions like usual. Her mom is a rocket scientist, and Robyn has been blessed with a fascinating mind.

During our talk, I used the phrase "do hard shit" multiple times. Finally, she asked, "So, what hard shit are you doing in your life right now?"

Uh, excuse me. I uh . . . um. My life had been hard enough up to this point.

I was stuck, and she knew it. I don't think she did it on purpose, but the glimmer in her eye made me realize she also knew she had hit me in the gut the way I was used to hitting people.

"I haven't been doing very much, and it's probably why I am as frustrated as I am."

Then it hit me. *Norway. Cold therapy.*

"I guess I need to change that," I said. "My buddy invited me to do something hard that I don't want to do, but you have made me painfully aware that I am supposed to do it."

I went into Norway feeling very skeptical, and when they gave us the schedule, I was even more frustrated. Over half the time was dedicated to indoor breathing exercises. How boring and dumb I thought. I rarely come away with much at most events like this and often contribute more than I receive. I sat in the back and was very reluctant in the beginning, but by the second evening, I realized that this was exactly what I needed at that moment of my life. It ended up being one of the most powerful experiences of my entire life. One of the biggest lessons I learned on that trip was that I needed to love the shit out of the hard stuff. In life, I often found a way to do the hard stuff, but always with a grit-my-teeth-and-bear-it mindset. What my "ice mom" taught me was how to love the hard and love the cold. By the end of the week, I was sitting in the freezing-cold water with a big smile on my face, as happy as a penguin.

One of the greatest advantages you can acquire—in life and in golf—is learning how to be comfortable in extremely uncomfortable situations. We may think our swing is messed up and in need of fixing, but in reality, what we really need is the ability to deal with uncomfortability. Competitive golf often comes down to who can be more comfortable being uncomfortable. Rarely are we going to hit it great or as great as we can. The big differentiator is the person who can accept it for what it is and do the best they can with what they have that day.

As Arnold Palmer once said, "Success in golf depends less on strength of body than upon strength of mind and character."

To help my clients work on this, I had them dress up crazy for regular activities, such as, trips to the grocery store. For most people, this is incredibly uncomfortable—which is exactly the point. Creating this kind of situation allowed my clients to learn to deal with those feelings in a very low-cost, low-risk situation.

My good friend Jim Murphy also happens to be a mental skills coach who teaches Inner Excellence® to a lot of guys on the PGA Tour. He has his clients do an exercise to help them master their ego, and specifically, get comfortable being uncomfortable. Just like the rest of us, PGA Tour players can be very self-conscious, concerned about chunking a chip, missing a short putt, or hitting a tee shot out of bounds. The exercise, which he calls, Alternate Target, involves (for tee shots), hitting a big hook or slice out of bounds to a specific target. Perhaps it's a tree in the woods or in the middle of a lake. The key is that you can't tell anyone that it was an alternate target. You have to sit in the awkward silence and learn to deal with the discomfort. Everything else is the same, pre-shot routine, specific target, etc.

The *thirty-minute drill* is another useful training exercise to work on dealing with uncomfortable feelings. In this exercise, you only get to hit ten balls on the range in thirty minutes. This is especially hard for college and pro players who have their names on their bags. They know people are watching them, and it's really weird to only hit one ball every three minutes. When you hit a bad one, the first thing you want to do is hit another one as quickly as possible to get that one out of your system. In competition, you have to sit with those feelings, so why not train to become more comfortable with them on the range. This drill also forces you to focus harder on each of those swings.

When you can hit hundreds of balls, you don't value each ball the same way you do when you only get to hit ten.

One of my former clients played professional golf and struggled with what other people thought of him. To help him, I had him hit a drastically different club off the tee than the other people he played with multiple times throughout his practice rounds. I ended up using this same strategy in our club championship.

I realized everyone hit driver on the par 5, second hole, and it made no sense. It is one of the only holes with out of bounds, and it was rare to get home in two. There is also a big slope that takes the majority of second shots down to a wedge distance from the green. It made no sense to bring on the risk of out of bounds with driver off the tee. So, I committed in my game plan that I wasn't going to hit driver. I was going to hit three wood, even though I had never seen anyone do this on the hole.

A guy who has won our club championship many times hit driver out of bounds on that very hole in the first round, and he ended up losing in extra holes to the guy I played in the finals.

I'm sure many other things make you incredibly uncomfortable but have virtually no real cost. Try and work on doing them until you slowly become more comfortable with the uncomfortable. I have a couple of cashmere hoodies that are my favorite clothing to wear while playing golf. During the semifinals of the club championship, my mom said to me, "Take your hoodie off! It's hot out."

I snapped at her, but later that night I realized something. Guys at the club were always getting frustrated when I wore pants and a hoodie when it was warm out. *It clicked.* This could be my secret weapon.

The morning of the finals, I woke up at 5:30 a.m., which was late for me during a tournament, and I went down to the sauna, as I do most mornings at home. This time though, I wore a hoodie. I sat in the sauna for twenty-five minutes, and I made a commitment to myself. No matter how hot it got that day—the forecast said the high would be eighty-four—my hoodie wasn't coming off for those thirty-six holes. I knew that every time my opponent looked at me, *it would make him sweat.*

I knew the finals would not be about who was the better golfer. Thirty-six holes of match play would come down to who was more comfortable being uncomfortable.

Where do you want to deal with large amounts of discomfort? It's a guarantee you are going to experience it, so where do you want to feel it?

I've found that people who get average results persist until they become uncomfortable. People who tend to get better results persist until things get very uncomfortable. But people who get world-class results have trained themselves to become extremely comfortable being uncomfortable. The only way to really grow is by being uncomfortable.

Strength is only built through resistance.

Soft roads create soft people.

Pressure is what you live for. If you are going to be successful in life, you are going to have pressure.
—Jack Nicklaus

CHAPTER 9

THE CLUB CHAMPIONSHIP

CONNECTING WITH HUMANS has always been a massive struggle for me. Growing up, sports were my only way to feel like I belonged, and at thirty-three years old, I found out I was on the autism spectrum. This cocktail of experiences resulted in a long-lasting core belief for me: *I was only valuable to others by being great at things.*

You might not like me, you might even hate me, but *you wanted me on your team.*

I only played team sports as a kid and I was a Ron Artest, Dennis Rodman type of competitor—intense and very in your face. When I first joined the country club, I told Scottie, "Golf is soft, and I'm gonna talk shit to all of you. None of this cheering for your opponent stuff."

After watching Scottie over four years and hundreds and hundreds of rounds, it finally clicked for me. That kind of attitude never worked in golf. It failed way more than it helped.

Golf is different.

The hardest person to beat is the guy who is nice, jovial, generous with rules, and full of dignity and class. Before our club championship, I decided that no matter the circumstances, I was going to play like Scottie. Win or lose, I was going to play with dignity and class. I wouldn't be making my opponent putt from inside two-feet or give the toughest rulings with drops or other rules. If I couldn't beat them without doing that, then I didn't want to win.

During the club championship, I was deferential and outwardly self-deprecating. I told every opponent I didn't have a chance against them and encouraged them. I even signed a couple of my books for one opponent with "Go win the whole thing!" Operating like this is incredibly challenging for me, but Scottie showed me that the toughest guy to beat is not the competitive jerk—it's the person you like so much you can't help but root for them.

Had you told me to do this even two or three years before winning our club championship I would have told you to go love yourself. But if I really was the competitive freak I believed, I had found a cheat code to be way more competitive: *Be the guy everyone wants to root for.*

That guy is really, really hard to beat.

Many of the guys I was playing in the club championship tried to cram for their matches. But as with a diet, test, or anything else, when you try to cram at the last minute, the likelihood of doing better than the person who has adopted it as a lifestyle is very low. Now, if you were a former Tour pro or played in college, that's a very different story. Those reps? Those are scary for someone with that type of experience and foundation.

For the rest of us? Either make practice a lifestyle or be content with where you are.

Maybe you can only commit to ten to thirty minutes a day. You might not be able to commit as much time as you'd like or that I or others can commit to. But I guarantee you *can* find a minimum of ten minutes a day. You *can* listen to guided imagery as you go to sleep. You *can* put a putting mat in your home or office and roll three to five balls three to eight times a day. You *can* do three to five mirror swings three times a day.

Will *you?* Most won't.

I encourage you to create a "Can Do List." What are all the things you can do to get better each week given your unique time and situational availability?

Everyone wants to be great until it's time to do what greatness requires. Everyone wants the end product without committing to the process. Everyone wants the results without the sacrifice. Forget your goals. *What are you willing to commit to doing during your 86,400 each day to close the gap between where your golf game is and where you want it to be? What are you willing to sacrifice inside your twenty-four hours to go from who you are to who you want to become?*

When I started playing in our big-money games, I was the worst at putting in the group. After three years of rolling balls consistently, I became one of the best putters in the club.

It's not magic. It's dirty, consistent work.

I knew I had put in that work. When I entered the club championship, I knew I was far from the best player in the field. In truth, I was probably the fifth or sixth best player in the field that year. A few of the best players at the club weren't able to play, so I knew that 2021 was probably my best chance at winning a club championship.

I had played in a lot of big-money games and lost. I was used to playing under a lot of financial pressure every single week. I knew most of the guys I would be playing against would be feeling the type of pressure that I felt multiple times a week. If I lost one of these matches, at least it wasn't going to cost me $1,500.

One of the coolest experiences in my golf life came when I was working with Laura Diaz. She was playing at Aviara, which was only a two-hour drive from my apartment in LA. She got a hole in one, and then on the next hole, she holed out for eagle from the fairway. The next day, on a different par three, she got another hole in one. On the next hole, she holed out for eagle from the fairway. Again. I couldn't believe it. It had never happened on the LPGA or PGA Tours, and I don't believe it has happened since.

One of the things we had worked on together was coming up with material for her to read during her downtime between shots. Most weeks I would send her five to ten pages of quotes and reminders to keep with her as she played.

Our club championship was the biggest tournament I had ever played in. It was also the first where I was truly alone. All of the tournament golf I had played up to that point was with a partner. This was going to be different, so I decided that I would make my own material to read while playing just like I had done for Laura. Competitive rounds of golf usually take around five hours to play, yet only two minutes of that is spent actually hitting the golf ball. That is a lot of downtime with your thoughts, and I decided that I needed to be intentional about fueling my heart with beneficial and constructive fuel, rather than just hoping I would remember all the things I teach.

For integrity's sake, I have copied and pasted the exact notes I had in my phone, as they were:

Whatever you are going to hit. Commit to it and swing with full conviction and live with the result.

Good width.
Sleeves under arms and stay connected.
Stay in the shot.
Get to my left heel more.
Slow takeaway.
Pull the handle.
Aim at left tree, and hit cut on one.
Every bounce we are going to love.
The toughest moments are an opportunity for special.
Flush the bad.
You are a rock, nothing gets to you.
Your swagger in the highs and lows is one of your greatest weapons. Your presence intimidates. You are Joshua Michael Medcalf. You impact the elements around you.
Love the shit out of everything.

You get to play.
The next moment isn't guaranteed.
Soak in and embrace this moment, it's all you got.
The bright lights are JMM's sanctuary.
You have been built for these moments.
Thank you Jesus for the opportunity to compete.
I have the wisdom of Solomon, the courage of David, and the love of Jesus.
You are loved.
You are enough.
Operate with that freedom.
Swing with the conviction that only comes from your value being constant and detached from the outcome.
Breathing exercises. Put hand over heart. What could you be grateful for in this moment?

I hadn't even planned on playing in our club championship because of all the golf legends that enter. Craig Davis won the Senior British Amateur and has won our club championship at least seven times. Tyler Gullikson has won many of the bigger amateur tournaments in the country and is one of the best amateur ball-strikers in the world. Jimmy Harris has won the club championship five or six times, and when he is on, he is as good as any PGA Tour pro. Jack Townsend is a young phenom who will be on the PGA Tour one day. Jacob Pilarski once went out and beat a group of six guys on four holes for a lot of money, using nothing but his seven iron against their full bag.

Jacob was the one who pushed the hardest for me to play. He had been deployed for seven months and was texting me all summer about it and worked extra hard to get home a little bit early to be able to play in the tournament.

The final motivator was a social dilemma that came up over the summer. One of the guys in the club had been dragging my name through the dirt. He didn't realize I was born in the dirt, and thrive there. All the shit he threw at me was the fertilizer I needed to blossom into a special golfer.

A few weeks before the tournament, I was playing with my buddies and one of them said, "You know the thing that will really drive him crazy? If you go out and win the club championship! He has always told people that he is going to be the 2028 club champ."

That was enough to get me off the fence.

A week before the qualifier, I went out and bought a more forgiving set of Miura irons that were the same model as my favorite club in my bag, a 52-degree old-school Miura wedge. I loved them, but on the Wednesday before the qualifier, I clicked one off the hosel with the five iron during a warm-up. I immediately took those clubs back to my truck and put my JPX 919s, back in the bag.

I was incredibly nervous the day of the qualifier and hit one of the worst shots of my life off the first tee. I normally have about ninety yards in, but after almost whiffing my tee shot, I had over two hundred yards left with trees to navigate. I hit another terrible shot—with my favorite club no less—and then chunked a chip. Thankfully, I had chunked it just enough to give myself a twenty-footer to save par. I missed, and tapped in for bogey, thankful that hole was over.

I kept hitting it poorly and made another bogey on number 3. After another terrible tee shot on four, I found myself stuck with another two-hundred-yard shot. This time, I finally woke up and swung with full conviction. My bad start allowed me to remember that I needed to actually surrender the outcome, and not just say it. In that moment I had a heart posture shift.

I then hit one of the best shots of my life. I nearly holed it, the ball lipped out. I had a one-foot tap in for birdie on the number 1 handicap hole. After that, I started hitting it more like myself, and after making par on the next couple of holes, I hit the ball inside ten feet on number 7.

I peeked at the leaderboard to see how far I had crawled back. The qualifer is stroke play, and I was tied for first.

Just then, the sky opened up and unleashed rain rarely seen in San Diego. It even hailed for a minute. We all went into the clubhouse, and after seeing a small river running through a few of the fairways, the head pro called it. The qualifier would be based on the holes that everyone had gotten through. The guy who I was tied for first with had made a double bogey on number 7, but it didn't matter. I would be the third seed, with Jimmy Harris having an automatic first seed as the reigning champ. I wasn't worried about my personal seeding, but I knew the tournament would be very messed up because, without eighteen holes for everything to shake out, some of the best players would be down at the bottom.

Sure enough, my first-round opponent was one of the guys I was most afraid of in the field—a real buzz saw. I knew this first match would be one of the toughest. My friend Jack Townsend, the young phenom, asked to caddy for me, and I welcomed his support.

My opponent hit his first approach shot to four feet and easily made birdie. Then he made a fifteen-footer for birdie on two. Thankfully, I made birdie to tie him on the second hole, but I knew I was in for a dogfight. He topped his tee shot on the par 3 third, but he still managed to tie the hole after I lipped out for par. He hit another one tight on five and made another birdie, so I was down two holes. The turning point in the match happened on the eleventh hole. We were tied, and I hit it to 1.5 feet.

It really was inside two feet, not the two feet people say when it's actually four to six feet from the hole. I expected him to concede the putt—but he didn't.

It was match play, and he was well within his right to make me putt it. But that lit a fire in me, and I knew what was coming.

I made it. On the next hole, he was in for par, and I had a twenty-five-foot par putt.

I bury it.

The next hole I hit it in the bunker and hit my bunker shot to twelve feet, and it's a snapper.

I bury it.

I hit a bad birdie putt on the following hole, which is the easiest par 5 in San Diego, and left myself a six-foot come back to tie the hole.

I bury it.

The next hole, I hit it to five feet. He missed his birdie putt.

I buried mine.

I was now up two, with three to play.

In 2012, I created the first mental training apps for basketball, soccer, and golf. They were very simple and included the ability to stream guided imagery mp3's. After a few years, we took them off the App Store because we didn't want to be a technology company and felt there were better options out there. But before our club championship, I found the golf guided imagery MP3 and listened to it a few times. One of the exercises in the audio is to clench every muscle in your body as tightly as you can—really squeeze every muscle in your body from your head to your toes—for fifteen seconds. Then you exhale, releasing a tremendous amount of tension from your body.

Going into the sixteenth hole that day, I could feel the tension rising in my body. This easy par 5 had caused me a lot of trouble over the years, and with only one hundred yards to the pin, I felt our tumultuous history together resurfacing.

In that moment, I decided to do a mini-version of the tense-everything in your body exercise. For just four to six seconds, I tensed everything in my body as hard as I could while standing. It was not as effective as laying down and going all out, but it still worked. I felt a lot of tension release from my body.

There is nothing stopping you from going a step further and lying down and doing this exercise in a round of golf. It's easy to go all out when you are lying down because you can tense everything up without worrying about falling over. But that wasn't what I did. Next time, I probably will.

I took a deep breath, made a half takeaway with good width, then swang with full conviction. It floated the bunker perfectly and left me with a twelve-footer for birdie. My opponent ended up three-putting and took off his hat. I never even had to putt.

I'd dodged a bullet. When everyone congratulated me after the round, I told them "I got lucky." The unlucky part was that my opponent the next morning would be the reigning senior club champ who had knocked off the legend, Craig Davis, to win the title. I saw him putting on the practice green and told him that I had no chance against him the following day. He had rolled through all the guys I played in big money games with in a year-long match play tournament, *and that was with strokes.* The next morning I would be playing him naked: *no strokes.*

Part of me telling him I had no chance was gamesmanship. I was taking all the pressure off of me and putting it on him. The other part, though, was cold hard facts. He is an incredible stick.

I had told my best friends, "If I am on, I can beat anyone not top fifty in the world." I had seen what I was capable of at the Macbeth, but golf is a funny game. It's very hard to be *on.* Sure, I had seen myself shoot five or six under on a nine, but putting it together at the right time—that would be tough to do under tournament conditions.

At the bar, I kept telling everyone that I got lucky and that I had no chance the following day. I was met with a barrage of insults about how stupid that was and how I had no chance with that kind of attitude. When I tried to explain the importance of surrendering the outcome, which I had written about in *Chop Wood Carry Water,* I was met with more eye rolls. I kept my mouth shut most of the time, but I occasionally let fly the reminder that they hadn't written the go-to book in sport psychology. I would trust myself over them.

Surrendering the outcome, in my opinion, is the most powerful philosophy and tool I have created, but I had never had the opportunity to put it into practice quite like I did in this tournament. In *Chop Wood Carry Water*, I wrote

"The ultimate illusion of the human experience is control."[8] *The person you want beside you in battle is the guy who has surrendered the outcome and surrendered to the fact that he might die. When you surrender the outcome, you are freed up to be at your best, to be in the moment, and to trust your training. It is the one who has surrendered the outcome who ironically has the greatest chance of survival.*

It is the one who has surrendered the outcome who has the greatest chance of success.

It is the one who has surrendered to the fact that he could fail who has the greatest likelihood of not failing.

Surrendering the outcome doesn't mean you care less about the outcome or your process. It doesn't mean you don't give your very best. It means that you have surrendered the outcome that is outside of your control. Many mornings I pray and surrender things that I desperately want to control but know I don't have control over. Surrendering the outcome is about having peace with that which is outside of our control without sacrificing the effort or care of what is inside of our control.

Until you surrender the outcome, you will always be the greatest enemy of your own success. In order to reach your greatest potential, you must operate with a heart posture of gratitude, commit to the controllables, surrender the outcome, and trust the process.

---

8 This gem came from Judah Smith.

Surrendering the outcome is especially important to me because I am hyperaware of my wiring. I am a competitive freak, so I never have to worry about competing hard—it's all I know how to do. Surrendering the outcome helps me to focus on the things I have 100 percent control over. Jack Nicklaus learned this lesson too: "I couldn't control Arnold Palmer, Gary Player, Tom Watson, or Lee Trevino. The only person I could control was me."

Self-awareness is crucial. If you are a people person, then you might need to focus hard on competing and less on surrendering the outcome. For those of us on the other end, we need to surrender and focus on people. If we don't, we can be miserable to play with and get in the way of our potential by trying to control the outcomes we can't control. It's like holding water in your hands. If you try and squeeze the water, it's going to shoot out the sides. You have to hold it carefully and gently. This applies in most areas of life. If my modus operandi is A, then I need to feel like I am doing Z, even if it feels uncomfortable. Even then, because of my wiring, I'm probably only adding a tiny bit of Z.

If we don't fight against our wiring, we can fall out of balance in life.

People who are grinders need to feel like they are spending too much time with friends and loved ones. Social people need to feel like they aren't spending enough time with people. Results-oriented people need to feel like they are completely focused on people. Even though it feels uncomfortable, the modus operandi that runs deep within us is always pulling us back toward our natural wiring.

The morning of the second round, I woke up at 3:00 a.m. after another terrible night of sleep. I slept maybe three and a half hours. I putted on my mat for a bit and then went to the sauna. After showering, I read a book and waited as the minutes crawled by. Finally, at 6:30 a.m., I left for *Stadium Golf* to hit balls. Due to the rain, our driving range was closed. I had a decent warm-up, but mostly it just felt good to hit some balls and remember that I could actually hit the ball in the air.

Earlier that summer, I had had night terrors about shanking it in a big gambling tournament coming up that July in Montana. Sure enough, in my second round, when I was two over through 16 holes and playing great, I clicked one off the hosel and sent it out of bounds.

It didn't happen again during the tournament, but it happened every time I went to the range, and it got so bad I stopped hitting balls before playing the rest of the tournament. It was so frustrating. I had worked so hard, and everything in my game felt so good. For months after, I still battled doubt, hesitation, and fear.

It wasn't as bad during the club championship, but every morning, I felt the nerves on those first few balls at the range. It was as if a hosel monster was going to jump up and bite me, even though that spring was the first time I'd dealt with them in four or five years.

On that first resurgence, I clicked one off the hosel at the range. *No need to panic*, I tried telling myself. *Then it happened again.* Then I couldn't not hit the hosel. I tried changing my grip. Nothing worked. All the PTSD from my past came flooding back.

I yelled over at Tyler Gullickson that I needed help. He came over and explained there's only one way to hit the hosel. "Just do this, and that won't be possible."

Even after trying to adjust, I hit five more in a row off the hosel. Tyler pulled out his phone and recorded one, stupefied. "When does Sam get back in town?" he asked.

"Not for two weeks."

He chose his words carefully. "I wouldn't play until then." He knew the gravity of what I felt, and after apologizing, he went back to his training. The anxiety I felt was immense, but still I played that day. Somehow, I shot 75. The monster never popped up on the course, but I could always feel it lurking. I can feel it while writing about it now. I hate even talking about it. It's very traumatizing for me.

Those first few balls on the range every morning before a match in our club championship were key for me. As crazy as it sounds, I needed proof I could hit the ball at a target.

I signed copies of *Chop Wood Carry Water* and *Pound the Stone* and gave them to my opponent when I got to the course that morning. My second-round opponent was the one I was most worried about. I'd even written "Go win the whole thing!" in his book. Truth is, I really meant it. I didn't think I stood a chance against him. He was too good and had way more high-level tournament experience, including big USGA tournaments. He played in college. He was the senior club champ. He was in great shape. And he hit it a mile.

I was going to need every edge I could get just to have a chance.

It all came down to the fifteenth hole. He was having a tough day, and I had been up 4 going into hole twelve. Then I lost two in a row. All the momentum was in his favor. We both hit bad shots to the toughest pin on fifteen. He hit a perfect bunker shot to a foot, and I conceded it. I hit a terrible chip and left myself an eighteen-footer to tie the hole. I looked at the putt for a couple of minutes, not having a clue what it would do. As I stood over it, I had a feeling that this putt was for the match. If I lost three in a row, it would be nearly impossible to close him out. But if I made the putt . . . I would probably win the match.

I settled on inside-right and let it roll. I hit a good putt, and it barely snuck in the side door. I let out a big sigh of relief.

The next hole is the same par 5 that I closed out my opponent on in the first round, and now we both have birdie putts from about thirteen feet. He is slightly closer. Two other guys are playing their match with us, and one of them has a putt on my line, so I'll get a read off his putt. Then the unthinkable happens: my buddy concedes the hole to the guy on my line. Now I'm putting blind. I know it has to move to my right, but I'm just not sure how much. I don't want to get too frisky because I need to guarantee a par.

I lip it out.

Throughout the round, my opponent had to make a lot of putts to stay alive, and he made a lot of them. They were always dripping just over the front edge of the hole, but I knew that would burn him at some point. Sure enough, he hit what looked like a perfect putt, but it stopped right on the lip, dead center of the hole.

We tied the hole, and now I'm up two with two to play.

We both hit solid tee shots and land on the green. A former legend on the PGA Tour, Billy Casper, said that if you are above the hole on seventeen, it's a hazard. Today it's a white pin, which is the most dangerous to be above. The middle tier is a shelf that's only about four feet when it's fast, and today it's very fast. I hit my approach just a bit too long and have a twenty-five-foot putt above the hole. He hit his birdie putt to four feet below the hole.

I breathe on my putt, and it trickled down to nine inches above the hole. I think the match is over, but he doesn't say anything.

I mark it.

He makes his par putt.

I'm still in a bit of shock that he hasn't taken off his hat, but put my ball down and knock it in.

I somehow have made it through the first weekend, and two incredibly tough opponents.

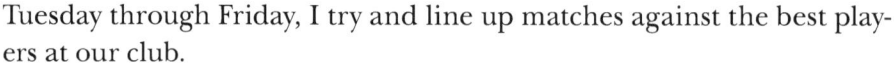

Tuesday through Friday, I try and line up matches against the best players at our club.

I suck.

I'm terrible.

I struggle to break 80.

On Friday, I play nine holes against one of our assistant pros, and I hit it so bad I could tell he felt sorry for me. He thought I had no chance the next day, it was written all over his face.

I texted Casey and told him I didn't know what was going on. It was as if everything had suddenly flipped in my golf world. I needed the bright lights to come alive. That was the only explanation I could think of. The alternative—that I had become terrible overnight—didn't make much sense.

Casey sent back a text that gave me chills. *"The bright lights are JMM's sanctuary!"* Tears are in my eyes now as I write this. Those words made it into my golf notes and never left.

When I first started speaking professionally, I struggled badly. Then I trained incredibly hard and put myself in really tough situations over and over again until I became world class at speaking onstage.

But something weird started to happen before I would speak. When I was trying to run through my stories in preparation for an event, stories that I had told thousands of times, I would go completely blank and could not remember them at all. It was the strangest thing. Then that led to nervousness about going blank in front of the audience. But then the bright lights would come on, and like magic, the stories would come flooding back, and I could deliver them with nuance and charisma.

"Maybe that's what has happened in golf?" I told a couple of close friends.

I hoped that was the case.

The week before the semifinals, I saw my opponent everywhere I went. When I went to hit at Riverwalk on Bob Townsend's *TrackMan*, he had just gotten a lesson and was there hitting balls. The next day when I got to the club, he was there grinding. The following day he was playing Tyler Gullickson as prep for our match.

I was curious, though, because I had seen him at a charity tournament a month before and he made it sound like golf wasn't really a priority for him. Now, all of a sudden, he was grinding like a Tour pro.

I had a sneaking suspicion that his cramming would backfire.

Golf is a cruel mistress, and she demands a lot from her lovers. She doesn't do well without a lot of consistency. If you try and cram she is likely to sabotage you.

I had asked a few people to caddy for me over the tournament, and everyone had been pretty flaky, so I was surprised when Jacob Pilarski was eager to be on my bag. My only hesitation was that as much as I loved him, we had never played together.

I'm an artist at heart, and my game is very confusing, to say the least. I don't play conventional golf by any stretch of the imagination, and that can be very confusing for great players. Casey calls me 'Bobby Filet' because even though we are the same height and similar build, I will routinely hit soft cuts or slinging slices. It's pretty common for me to hit a four or five iron on a hole where he hits an eight or a nine.

I felt incredibly honored that a player of Jacob's caliber would want to be on my bag. The only thing I made Jacob commit to was my philosophy of surrendering the outcome.

Ben Hogan once said, "Golf is 20 percent talent and 80 percent management." But for most rounds of golf at San Diego Country Club, I don't have a game plan. Sam has taught me how to manage my game well, and I think I make good decisions, but I had never mapped out a course with a complete game plan until our club championship. Ninety yards is my best number, so Jacob and I were incredibly intentional about trying to get to that yardage as many times per round as possible.

On the first hole of the semifinals, my opponent came out on fire. He got three looks at his birdie putt on number 1 from me and the other guys, and then he buried his.

I barely missed from thirty feet.

On the second hole, he almost holed his eagle chip but had to settle for a tap-in birdie. He was up two.

I walked over to my cart, smiled at my mom, and said, "Now all the pressure is on him. Let's see how he handles it." By the ninth hole, I was up two, and my putter was *en fuego*. By the fourteenth hole, I made another birdie, and it was over. I won the match 5&4.

I was headed to the finals.

The guy I would be playing was a former head pro from a couple of different clubs on the East Coast. He had beaten the legend, Jimmy Harris, and my buddy Jacob Pilarski, the two guys who had been in the finals the year before.

I was struggling with cognitive dissonance. What was happening felt so sureal. I had been a 5 handicap for most of the summer, and now four months later I was a +3. It was hard to believe. Was it real, or was I in a movie? Was it really possible to have made such a drastic jump so quickly?

For three years, my handicap was always the lowest around the same time of year as our club championship, but the lowest it ever got to was a 1.3 index, or a 3 handicap from the blue tees at our club.

To make it even harder psychologically, my nemesis had been telling everyone in the club I was a sandbagger. To be fair, my unheard-of improvement certainly looked suspicious.

Jealousy is a destructive drug.

The thing I kept reminding myself was that this wasn't the first time this had happened in my life. In fact, it matched the pattern of my life in every area. It happened at Duke with soccer. It happened in my speaking career. It happened in my writing career. And now it was happening in golf.

I love sleep, and typically it comes very easily to me. It's how I process, but before tournaments, sleep is very hard to come by.

Before the qualifier and every match leading up to the finals, I barely slept, and then the strangest thing happened. The night before the finals, I slept like a baby. I got almost seven hours of solid sleep.

On my way into the club that morning, I was overcome by emotion. It's hard to explain if you've never felt something like this, but I knew I was going to win our club championship that day. I didn't think it in my head. I felt it deep within my heart.

But that wasn't what made me emotional.

It was Scottie. I realized early in the tournament that I wanted to win it for him. He had done so much for our club and so many of the members. He had done so much for me personally, and I wanted to do it for him.

I was crying on my way in because I felt that my winning could help get Scottie back to the club. Some messed-up stuff had happened, and I wanted to try and mend fences. We needed Scottie back at the club. I needed Scottie back at the club. He was my golf mentor, and I was going to go out and win it for him. Then I would use my new clout at the club to try and get him back where he belonged.

Through the first seventeen holes, the momentum was in my favor. I was up six holes, and we both had putts from about twelve feet for par on 18. The big challenge for me was the greens. A computer glitch had resulted in the greens accidentaly getting watered the night before, and then the guy in charge of rolling the greens didn't show up. The balls were only rolling at 11.5 instead of 13's like they were the day before. This made lag-putting easier, but holing putts much harder.

I left my putt dead in the heart a couple of rotations short, and then for the first time all day, he made a putt to win a hole. We then had a forty-five-minute break for lunch before the final eighteen holes.

My driver had started to feel wonky the last few holes, and I could feel myself getting handsy. During the break in between rounds, I FaceTimed Sam and had him watch my swing and give feedback. I decided I was going to move to my go-to shot, an outside takeaway with a hard cut that just gets the ball in play and put the pressure on the more steady part of my game.

People had started to show up to watch the end of the match, and everything just felt off when we started back up. I was no longer in the flow state I had been in for the first eighteen holes. Jacob said to me as we drove to the first hole, "Just keep hitting greens in regulation, two-putt, and we will be fine." He had only seen me play great up to that point; he didn't really understand that I'd been playing out of my mind. This wasn't the way I normally played.

I took a deep breath and smiled. "You know, Jake, that would be awesome, but I'm not sure I can keep hitting the ball like I have been under this kind of pressure. And the funny thing is, that's not my game. My game is built on being a cockroach and getting up and down from places no one ever should. As nice as it would be to hit greens in regulation and have casual two-putts, what will really crush him psychologically is if I start missing greens and get up and down."

In those pressurized moments, it's crazy how much you can hear, especially when you aren't in a flow state and pull your tee shot behind your nemesis tree on the first hole. The pin was on the far-right ridge in the middle of the green. My only hope was to hit it way left to avoid hitting the tree and pray to have a putt at it. I had 104 yards, and I was sitting in some thick rough. I pulled out my gap wedge.

I went through my routine, and right as I started my takeaway, I heard my buddies Zack and Gareth whispering and laughing like little schoolgirls. The wild thing was, they were ninety yards away, but it felt like they were standing right beside me. I stopped at the top of my swing and backed away from the ball. I turned around and shot them a death stare.

They would later tell me that they couldn't even fathom that I could hear them, given how far away they were. But they quieted up, and I hit the shot exactly how I wanted to, but I was now left with a treacherous putt down a ridge from fifty feet. I drove over to my buddies and curtly told them that although I was thrilled they were there to support me, they needed to "kindly shut up while we are over the ball." They apologized and promised to behave.

Now, if I missed my line by just a foot on either side, or if my speed was even a little off, I could end up with a thirty-footer or more for par. Meanwhile, my opponent had a birdie putt straight up the hill from twenty five feet.

Thankfully, I hit a perfect putt and cozied it up a few inches from the hole. My putt was conceded. My opponent hit a good but, but just missed. We tied the hole.

Hole 2 is the par 5 I committed to hitting three wood on, but at the last second, I told Jake, "If I'm gonna hit the safe shot, I might as well hit the *really safe* shot." I asked him for my five wood and hit a bunt shot that maybe went 175 yds down the far left side.

I heard audible gasps from the small crowd that had formed. A former club president would later tell me he thought I was crazy when he saw me hit that shot. "Nobody does that!"

But I didn't get where I was in life by doing what everyone else does. I'd always colored outside the lines.

I got up to my ball, and while it might have looked terrible from the tee, I had a fluffy lie with a beautiful angle to rip a three wood over the ridge.

I smoked my three wood down the right side perfectly, leaving myself about 110 yards to a back pin. My competitor pulled his approach into the left rough and had a virtually impossible up-and-down for par.

I hit a conservative shot that just missed the back ridge and left me a forty-footer up the ridge. I thought I hit a good putt, but it came up five feet short with at least a cup and a half of break for the next one. I wasn't too worried, though, because my opponent was facing a death chip.

Then he hits a PGA Tour–quality shot. It bounces twice in the rough and trickles past the hole. He buried the ten-foot come backer for par.

Suddenly I was forced to make a slider to *tie the hole* when the whole time I was thinking it would be to win the hole. If I missed, I would only be up four, and the momentum would have swung back in his favor. *"It's okay,"* I told myself. *"You lost this hole already, so just put a good stroke on it."* After surrendering the putt, I smiled as I took a deep breath, then hit it. It felt great coming off the face, but I didn't want to peek early. I looked up as it hit the back of the cup.

I gave my mom and Jake a cheeky smile as I picked my ball out of the hole.

The next hole was one of the toughest par 3s in Southern California: 246 yards from the tips, with bunkers guarding the green on both sides. A former president of our club who I had never met pulled up and said, "You are a good player."

I smiled and said deferentially, "No, my opponent is a good player."

He looked me dead in the eyes. "No, you are a good player. He is a *great* player!"

Uh, thanks?

Right on time, my opponent stepped up and hit a perfect shot to sixteen feet pin-high.

I looked at Jake and told him, "Well, we lost this hole." I proceeded to hit a terrible shot, short-siding myself behind a bunker with a virtually impossible chip. The back of the bunker runs away from me, so I only have a three-foot landing zone to get it really close.

It's funny some of the things that give you momentum, and it was at that moment my fellow cockroach brother, Casey, showed up. As soon as I saw him, I got new wind in my sails. I don't recommend doing this, but I gave him the cockroach antennae as I walked over to my ball. I hit a good chip, but not a great one. I left myself with a fifteen-foot par putt down the hill.

While my opponent was reading his putt, Jake walked up to me and asked, "What do you see?" Intentionally loud enough for my opponent to hear it, I told him, "I got it! I made this putt last week!"

My opponent hit his putt to 4.5 feet, outside of range for me to concede it.

Unbeknownst to me, at that moment Casey said to Gareth and Zack, "These are the ones he makes, and they are absolute backbreakers!" I took a deep breath and whispered to myself, "Thank you for the opportunity to compete." I took one last look at the line and pulled the trigger. As soon as I looked up, I knew I buried it. It was on a perfect line, and even from ten feet out, I knew it was perfect speed.

I didn't even need to watch what was coming next. *I already knew.*

My opponent lipped out. All hope and optimism melted from his face in that moment. We had more holes left, but it was over.

I buried a birdie putt on hole 7 and was up seven. I then hit a ridiculous seven-iron shot from under a tree from ninety-seven yards, leaving me eight feet beneath the hole for a birdie putt on number 8. He conceded the hole after hitting it in the water. I was up eight with ten holes to play.

I started having fun with my friends and just enjoying the moment. I don't care if you are the best player in the world—you aren't beating me on eight out of ten holes on my home course.

I sure made it interesting, though. I chunked my tee shot on the eleventh hole, made bogey, and lost the hole. On number 12, he made me putt a par putt from fourteen inches, and I missed it. After he made me putt that one, I got really mad and locked back in for the next two holes. After a few great shots, it was over for real. I won the 2021 San Diego Country Club Championship up six with four holes to play. My buddies soaked me in champagne, and it was an amazing feeling.

It felt too good to be true.

It felt like a movie.

Even though I knew I was going to win that morning on the way in, it still felt surreal to be soaked in champagne.

As soon as I had taken the pictures for the club, I called Scottie and told him what had happened that morning coming into the club, how grateful I was for his mentorship, and how sorry I was for what had happened to him. He told me that he loved me and was very proud of me.

THE BOYS SPRAYING ME WITH CHAMPAGNE ON THE FOURTEENTH HOLE.

GETTING A HUG FROM MY FELLOW COCKROACH BROTHER.

EMO ZACK APOLOGIZING FOR WHAT HAPPENED ON THE 19TH
HOLE AND TELLING ME HOW PROUD HE IS OF ME.

IT WAS REALLY SPECIAL HAVING MY MOM GET TO WATCH THE TOURNAMENT.

JACOB PILARSKI AND I AFTER WE WON.

JAKE AND I TRYING TO COOL OFF WITH THE FAN.

Just two cockroaches in Lake Tahoe playing some G. You
might notice my smile is much bigger than his—I had just
cockroached him real dirty on the seventeenth hole.

CHAPTER 10

TWELVE FEET AND IN

ONE HUNDRED YARDS from the hole is where you gain or lose a lot of strokes, especially if you have to putt everything out. Everything in golf is important, but the majority of people waste way too much time banging balls on the range in ways that rarely translate to the course.

When really good players see me hit it, they think, *This guy has no chance against me.* But then I do what I normally do: plod along like a tortoise or, as the SoCal GOAT says, "you par people to death!"

When I was growing up, people asked me what drills they could do to get a better touch in soccer. They hated my response. I would tell them to juggle a soccer ball with their feet for one to two hours a day. No fancy drills, just a lot of time touching the ball.

When I was living in LA and asked a friend who played college golf for some good putting drills, I shouldn't have been surprised when she looked at me with annoyance and said, "There are no fancy drills to make you better at putting. It's just a lot of time spent hitting putts. The more you putt, the better your feel."

This reminds me of what happened with nine Michigan hospitals in 2004 that experimented with a new protocol.[9] In the midst of one of the greatest technological and scientific periods in history, these hospitals saved over 1,500 lives, reduced infection rates by 66 percent, and saved over $75 million. They did all of this in less than eighteen months, and they didn't do it with any fancy new technology or science.

---

9 https://jamesclear.com/checklist-solutions

How did they do it? They followed a simple checklist protocol. The number one thing on the checklist was to have every single person wash their hands before entering the operating room. This was 2004! Ignaz Semmelweis discovered the power of fighting disease with handwashing back in 1847!

For all our obsession with innovation, we often miss the power in doing the unremarkable with remarkable consistency. *Knowing the power of something doesn't mean that we actually do it.* When I am playing, I forget to do many of the things I teach professional golfers and have written about in best-selling books!

To unlock the power of a tested method, you have to commit to doing it—*and then actually do it every time.* The doctors, nurses, and staff in those hospitals knew the power of washing their hands, but it wasn't until they created a protocol to do it every single time. *Then* they got those incredible results. C.S. Lewis said, "when you put first things first, secondary things aren't suppressed, they increase." It's tempting in the world we live in to focus on secondary things like goals and results, but there is tremendous power when we simply focus on putting first things first.

The golf technology in both clubs and feedback machines is astounding, and I use some of those things for my game. But there are so many little things that cost virtually no money that can help us get better and bring out our best.

In my opinion, putting is the washing of hands for golf. It is the great differentiator in the game that most people spend little time on. It costs money for range balls. It costs money for lessons. It costs money to get fitted for clubs. It costs money to hit on a TrackMan. It costs money to play a round. But chipping and putting? You can go out and do those for free. While a putting mat does cost money, it is a nominal one-time cost that allows you to "wash your hands" every single day for as long as you want.

San Diego Country Club is known for having some of the fastest greens in the world. Xander Schauffele typically spends time at our club before Augusta to get ready for the Master's greens.

I know that when we have tournaments our greens are going to be any-where from twelve to fourteen on the Stimpmeter. That's like putting on glass. The other day I invited a teaching pro from Twitter to come down and play, and a random person chimed in. "Make sure you putt on hardwood floors before you go, because that's what it's gonna be like putting there."

My putting mat at home is on my hardwood floor and is super-tight, rolling around a fourteen or fifteen. Of course, training this way means, I am going to have a harder time on slower greens—as my fellow cock-roach brother loves to say, "everyone knows Medcalf can't putt on slow greens!" But my training is to prepare me for tournaments. Does putting at home still help me on slower greens? It certainly helps more than no training, but I'm keenly aware that the type of training I do prepares me for lightning-fast greens. During our club championship, I missed maybe two putts over four rounds that I should have made, and nothing inside eight feet for par except the fourteen-inch putt on the thirtieth hole of the final match when I was up so much it didn't matter.

When do you want to be at your best with putting? Make sure that your training reflects that in the type of mat and greens you practice on.

The one place I do more block practice than random practice is at home. In order to build in some elements of random practice, I hit putts at dif-ferent spots on the mat, never hitting the same putt twice. I also hit very few putts straight down the line. Sam has told me that it is almost like cheating when you putt parallel to the mat. There are no parallel lines on a real green, so I always try to putt at angles on the mat.

Many of my friends complain about their putting, and I tell them, "Stop complaining, get the mat,[10] and start rolling balls on it *every single day.*" The one time my putting got off was when I spent six months as a nomad living out of hotels. Sometimes I would roll my matt out in the hotel, but

---

10 The putting mat that I use is listed on Amazon as the *"SKLZ Vari-Break-adjustable putting green."* I threw away the pads underneath and put the mat flat on the hard-wood floor.

the mat just isn't the same on carpet. As soon as I got a new place and started rolling them again, my putting came right back.

Benjamin Hardy wrote a great book called *Willpower Doesn't Work*. In it, he shares how research has shown that environment trumps willpower. Our environment shapes us more than anything. That is why product placement in stores is so important. When managers moved water to the front of the store, near the checkout lines, water purchases increased by around 25 percent.

We often think we need more willpower to make better choices, but our immediate environment impacts our choices more than anything. Rather than trying to rely on your willpower, what do you need to put in your immediate environment to help you become more of the person you want to become? What do you need to remove from your environment to become more like that person?

When I put out early drafts of this book, I had quite a few devout followers of Scott Fawcett come at me hard over this chapter. It was good, it forced me to think deeper, and talk to more people I trust about what matters most.

Here's the deal, the easiest, least expensive, and fastest way for most hacks to shave strokes off their game is by working on putting and short game. Now, am I biased towards putting because my home course as super slick greens that Xander uses as training for The Masters? Yes.

Our club is a second shot golf course that puts a premium on short game. You can hit it almost anywhere off the tee, and still have a chance at birdie with a great approach.

So, depending on the type of course(s) you play the most, distance and accuracy off the tee matter differently. However, most amateurs spend more than 90% of their "practice" on the driving range. Tour players spend 50-70% of their time on short game.

Ben Pellicani summed it up well, "Ball striking and accuracy are the price of admission, putting wins tournaments."

Would I rather have a wedge in my hand than a six iron? Every time.

Do I consistently beat people that have a 3-4 club advantage on me? All the time.

Extra distance is incredible, and I have worked hard to gain some of that.

Accurate extra distance is the best. But putting is still king, because no matter how far you hit it, in real golf, you have to get the ball in the hole. When the next one matters, and you can't just scoop your ball, putting can be incredibly hard. I've watched guys four putt from two feet on tough greens. Stroke play tournament golf is a different animal. People miss from inside a foot.

The other thing that isn't going to show up in the fancy 'distance vs putting stats' people post online is the momentum you gain from making a putt. The reverse is also true, there's little as deflating as smoking a drive, stuffing it inside five feet, and then misssing the birdie putt. It's even tougher when you walk away with bogey or worse.

One of the most challenging people to play against is the person who hits it 220 yards down the middle. They can't reach the green, so they hit their five-wood twenty yards short, and then they bump it up inside ten feet. Then they make the putt. If you haven't gotten smoked by this player, then you haven't played much golf. No one is more psychologically challenging to play.

Distance is great! I'll always take a wedge in over a long iron, but accuracy is more important than length, and the great equalizer will always be the flat stick.

CHAPTER 11

THE PATH TO MASTERY

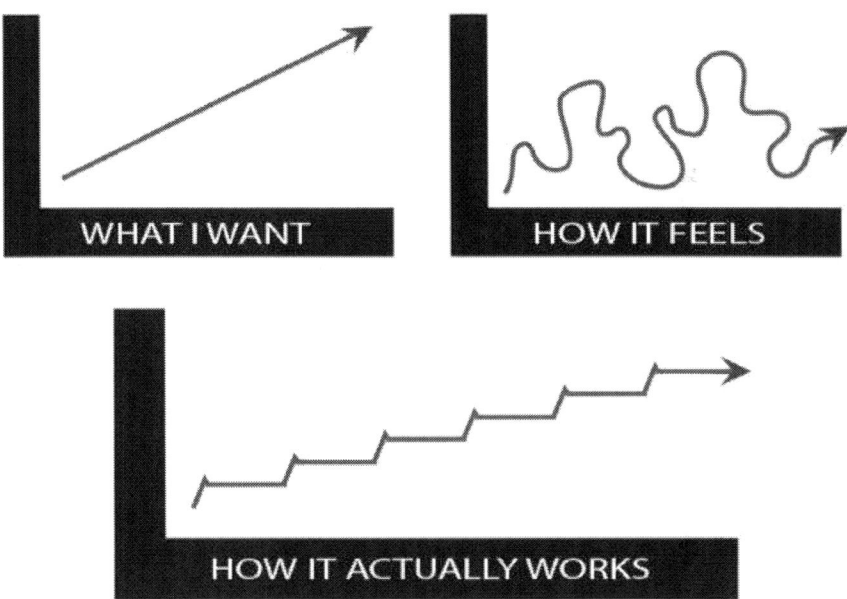

The path to mastery[11] is a lot of things, but it's not a straight line.

You know the other surprising thing about mastery? While mastery itself is an incredible thing, getting there isn't actually that exciting. Excellence is mundane.[12] There is nothing flashy about doing the hard work in the

---

11 For more on mastery, read my book *Pound the Stone: Seven Lessons to Develop Grit on the Path to Mastery.*

12 For more on this, read "The Mundanity of Excellence" by Daniel F. Chambliss

dark while the rest of the world is asleep. There's nothing sexy about putting in hard work for years, trying and failing to master your game.

Golf is such a rollercoaster. Six weeks after winning the club championship, my partner and I finished dead last in a member guest tournament at our club. There are times when it feels like the game is easy, and you are going to be great forever. Other days it feels like I want to quit and that I should never waste another second playing.

I have to constantly remind myself that the path to mastery is a never-ending journey, and I need to stay focused on the fundamentals.

At San Diego Country Club, there is one constant. Members, head and assistant pros, general managers, staff, and superintendents have cycled through over the last thirty years, but the legendary player Craig Davis is always there. Craig bought a house next to the second hole at our club over thirty years ago, and almost every evening you will see him out hitting balls and on the putting green.

Greatness isn't sexy. It is hard, dirty work.

WHEN ARE YOU AT YOUR BEST?

IN MOST AREAS of my life, I vacillate between being super-quick to trust my gut or am super deliberate, studying everything to account for each variable. With golf, I prefer the methodical nature of tournament golf because I get to really take my time. I tend to play my best golf when I'm intentional. The more looks I have from each side of a putt, the better I am.

Two mistakes my club championship opponents made were walking the golf course and not using a caddie. I used all the rules to my benefit. While they were burning energy walking the course and having to second-guess their reads, I had way more time to analyze each shot and have them double-confirmed by my caddie.

It doesn't matter when you play at your best. What matters is that you are aware of it and can catch yourself when you start doing the opposite. Most people are way more talkative when they are playing well. When they are playing poorly, they get quiet and often stuck in their head.

I don't think one is better than the other; it's just vital to know when you are at your best and fight your default tendencies when you are struggling. You can't control when you get bad breaks or don't hit it as well as you would like, but you can control your body language, your focus, how fast or slow you play, and how talkative you are.

Remember, the key is to focus all your energy on the things inside your control and surrender everything that's outside of your control.

We also need to train against our frustrations. Jack Nicklaus said, "Ask yourself how many shots you would have saved if you always developed a strategy before you hit, always played within your capabilities, never lost your temper, and never got down on yourself." If you hate slow play,

I want you to play one round a week with the slowest player you know. If you hate playing with people who talk too much, I want you to play one round a week with the most talkative person you know. If you hate playing in silence, I want you to play one round a week with the quietest person you know.

It doesn't matter what drives you crazy. If you are training for highly competitive golf at any level, than you should train against what drives you crazy every week. Ideally as much as possible and in worse conditions than you would encounter in competition.

We want to make our training so hard that competition feels easy.

Where do you experience extreme discomfort? It's a guarantee you are going to feel it, and the choice you have is to experience it in training or under the bright lights of competition. Don't get exposed by the bright lights. Know your weaknesses, and train against them.

How have you trained in the past? Do you make your training tougher than a competition?

Under pressure, you don't rise to the occasion. You sink to the level of your training.

CHAPTER 13

PERFORMANCE CUE CARD

A PERFORMANCE CUE card is a helpful tool we have created for our clients. Typically we have them make it on a notecard and laminate it to keep in their pin sheet or somewhere with their key reminders.

When I was working on this book, I found one I had created for myself stashed in one of my old journals.

At the top, I have my vision for myself at this event. These are things I want to focus on that are controllable. When you make your own performance cue card, everything written down should be close to 100 percent controllable—not arbitrary outcomes that you lack control over.

Beneath your vision/mission should be beneficial and constructive self-talk statements. Think about what a great coach would say to you after a mistake, then write those things down as reminders of what to say to yourself after a mistake. This can save you from beating yourself up with negative self-talk.

It is difficult to see the opportunity for special in front of you and play present when you are focused on past mistakes.

Tiger Woods said, "You've got to stay patient, stay in the moment, and keep grinding. You never know what can happen."

Ben Hogan felt similar, and said "The most important shot in golf is the next one."

Next on the card, you want a picture or a word that reminds you to shift your focus. For me, that is my little brother Luke. He has cerebral palsy and can't walk, talk, or feed himself. He has an incredible outlook on life even though he can't do things I take for granted every single day.

Next, you want to pick a song with lyrics you can hum to yourself as you play. The lyrics that you sow into your heart should be beneficial and constructive. This song is different than a trigger song. These lyrics should be a high level of intentional self-talk. This is a way of playing offense with mental training and sowing beneficial and constructive fuel into your mind and heart. Most people only use mental training to play defense when things are going poorly. It is good to have the mental skills to navigate those situations and have B&C self-talk statements for when we make mistakes, but we want to play offense as well.

With this in mind, write down on your card a time when you really crushed it at something. A time that when you think about it, it brings back awesome feelings of joy and conviction. This can be a source of strength and a reminder of the power you have inside you.

Lastly, you want to have your warrior dial—a number that indicates your peak performance state for this specific event. You might even want to have three different numbers. One for the start, one for the middle, and one for the end of the round. This number correlates to when you are at your best. Ten is super hyped up and a bit crazy. Zero is so stoic you might be near death. Everyone is different, and you need to figure out when you are at your best. Then consider things you can do to amp yourself up or pull yourself back down, depending on what you need in the moment.

What you need to do to be at peak performance is contextual. When we had clients who were playing an "easier" opponent on a Tuesday, they often needed to get way more amped up for that match. When they were playing on Friday night on ESPN against a top opponent, they needed to meditate, do deep-breathing exercises, and listen to slow classical music.

I wish I had learned about this when I was playing in high school and college. I thought you were always supposed to get hyped up before games, so I would watch a movie like *Braveheart* and listen to hardcore rap music. Not surprisingly, I got a lot of red cards because my peak performance number was probably a 6 or a 7, but I was always red-lining at a 10. I was wasting vital energy and had a hard time staying on the field from cramping when I wasn't getting ejected from games.

Again, it's not about what is right or wrong, but rather developing more self-awareness around when you are at your best.

T2BC Performance Cue Card

100% Controllable Mission for This Round

_____

_____

100% Controllable Keys to Success

1. _____

2. _____

3. _____

4. _____

Beneficial and Constructive Self-Talk Statements

* _____

* _____

* _____

Better Perspective Word or Picture Reminder

Peak Performance Numbers One experience where you absolutely crushed it:

Beginning of round: _____

Middle of round: _____

End of round: _____

Beneficial and Constructive Song Lyrics to Sing/Hum to Yourself

_____

_____

Key Reminders for Your Round

Whatever you are going to hit, commit to it and swing with full conviction.
We are going to love every bounce.
The toughest moments are opportunities for special.
You *get* to compete today.
The next moment is not guaranteed. Soak it in and embrace this moment. It's all you are promised.
Swing with the conviction that comes from knowing your value isn't attached to this round or shot.
You are loved. You are enough.
If you start to feel tension building in your body, tense all your muscles as hard as you can for five to ten seconds, then let it all out.

Visit **www.t2bc.com/hack** for a printable WWW pin sheet journal, performance cue card, and good reminders.

CHAPTER 14

IDENTITY

WHEN I DO a workshop for a team or give a keynote, I'll often start by taking out a thick fifteen-foot chain and wrapping it around my neck and body. I tell the audience that our value comes from who we are and that every human being is infinitely priceless.

The lie that society tries to make us believe is that our value comes from what we do and how we perform. While the amount of money, playing time, and such might depend on our performance, our intrinsic value is stable. It never goes up or down. But when we believe the lie that our value comes from what we do and not from who we are, it's like wrapping that big heavy chain around our necks and trying to go out and do what we've trained to do.

When we live in the Truth, we can take that heavy chain off our necks, freeing our training to do its work instead of being choked out by lies.

When facing a tough tee shot, I try and remind myself that I am loved and that my value doesn't come from how I hit the shot. Then I take a deep breath—and let it go. When I do this, I tend to hit much better shots than when I hit a shot believing the lie that my value and identity are somehow anchored to the results.

CHAPTER 15

THE PERFECTIONISM MYTH

This is a game of misses. The guy who misses the best is going to win.
—Ben Hogan

ONE CHALLENGE FOR many people in golf is the myth of perfectionism. Perfectionism is one of the most dangerous things you can believe in when it comes to unleashing your full potential in golf and life. Most of it is ego. *Ego is a ravenous beast that poisons everything it encounters, no matter the achievements it's enabled. Ego might get some things done, but it ruins a lot of what really matters along the way.*

When we empty ourselves of ego and fear, we make room for love, peace, contentment, joy, and courage. This is one of life's greatest challenges because so many people around us, especially those in leadership positions, operate from their ego instead of their heart. We must empty our ego daily so we can fulfill our potential rather than being ruled by our lowest self.

Claiming to be a perfectionist is just another way of saying you're afraid:

Afraid of being exposed

- Afraid of not being good enough
- Afraid of letting people down
- Afraid of reaching your limits

Expecting perfection smothers your progress by convincing you to play it safe by avoiding the necessary mistakes that will help you grow.

When we are learning to walk, we learn how to fall, and that is how we get better and better. With each fall, you got a little bit better at tumbling in a way that wasn't quite as painful. Your body learns what to do when you lose your balance to minimize the pain and increase the likelihood that you can stabilize. As a result, you were able to spend more time on your feet practicing the task you were trying to master: walking.

When learning to play great golf, especially tournament golf, productive failure is not just okay—it's an expectation! If you never fail, you are not pushing the edges of your ability, and that's the only way you can maximize your growth.

Perfectionism is a defense mechanism to minimize the judgment of others and your own exposure to failure. It's a label that turns into an excuse for you to hide behind so you can play small and never have to feel inadequate. But without failure, there is no growth.

If you only take on tasks, shots, opponents, and tournaments where you are confident you can succeed, you will never truly know your potential. You can't keep trying to avoid failure. You need to start pursuing it head-on.

People who call themselves perfectionists think their achievements come from paying deep attention to detail. They think they have high standards for themselves, but hiding behind these tendencies is a desire to control things to eliminate the potential pain of failure and judgment. If they really were trying to get closer to perfect or their greatest potential, they would try at minimum to triple their rate of productive failure.

People who think they're perfectionists are hiding behind a mask, afraid of being exposed as a fraud. When we fall into perfectionism mode, we're trying to protect our ego. But here's the reality: perfectionism kills our potential by robbing us of the ugly reps—the ones we need most.

A wise person once said,

The graveyard is the richest place on earth because it is here that you will find all the hopes and dreams that were never fulfilled, the books that were never written, the songs that were never sung, the inventions that were never shared, the cures that were never discovered, all because someone was too afraid to take that first step, persist and keep at it, long after the masses told them to throw in the towel.

Don't let your greatness die within you because of fake perfectionism that's just trying to protect your ego. Start viewing failure as the price of admission for the opportunity to chase your dreams.

When we operate from a place of wholeness and unconditional love, knowing our identity and worth are not based on the results of our performance, we are freed up to empty the tank and play with joy. We *get* to play and we *get* to truly live.

If you need a good perspective check, visit some people in a hospital or a cancer ward who have lost the ability to do the things we take for granted every single day.

We *get* to play.

We *get* to compete.

It's a privilege, and it can disappear in the blink of an eye.

CHAPTER 16

REWIRING YOUR BRAIN

I wrote this book, in part, because of a conversation I had with Sam after winning the club championship. He told me one of the most important things I shared with him was a few weeks before when I reminded him to do his What Went Well (WWW) journal on his pin sheet during tournaments. I got frustrated and said, "That is in *Chop Wood Carry Water*! You read that book four years ago!"

He told me that in *Chop Wood Carry Water*, I say to do WWW journaling after your training session or competition. I realized that while most of our Train to Be Clutch "secrets" are in our books, there are nuances to each sport that I only share with teams and athletes when I am in those specific contexts. Most of what I have written in my eight books is generic and requires readers to experiment with the ideas and tools in their own sport or business.

WWW journaling is especially important for those who struggle with belief and are very hard on themselves. When I was working with Laura Diaz, she found great value in WWW journaling on her pin sheet in between holes. It's a great way to create momentum in your game.

Think about this. Let's say you stripe a drive down the middle, stuff a wedge to two feet, but then miss the putt. What are you thinking about as you walk to the next tee? Most people are thinking about the missed putt instead of thinking about everything they did well to get to that spot. It even happens to the best: "Like most . . . I have a tendency to remember my poor shots a shade more vividly than the good ones" -Ben Hogan.

WWW journaling is about redirecting our focus to what we did well, instead of allowing the bad to carry more weight. The people in my life know how important this is for me and are used to me doing this out loud.

However, it is still more beneficial to be deliberate and intentional about writing it out. I believe I would have greatly benefitted from doing this exercise during my final round at *The Macbeth*. I should have been focused on the amazing shots I was hitting and how good I was putting, instead of allowing my focus to get fixated on the one two-foot putt that I missed.

It is much easier for our brains to focus on the negatives, even if they are actually totally outweighed by the stuff we do well.

Let me tell you a couple of secrets about how our marvelous brains work. I had the privilege of studying under Dr. David Rubin at Duke. He is one of the world's foremost authorities on autobiographical memory.

Our memories are not created through experiences. Rather, they are created through the stories we tell ourselves and others about those experiences. If you leave practice or a round and you tell everyone how poorly you played and you focus on all your mistakes, that is what your brain will remember. Most people undermine all the hard work they put in by telling negative stories and blocking out all their growth.

Our brains are marvelous machines that process around eleven million bits of information per second. However, we are only *aware* of about forty of those bits. That means you are only aware of 0.00000364 of what is actually happening around you!

We block out the other 99.99999 percent of what our brain is processing.

If we want to adopt a more beneficial and constructive lens, we must start rewiring the way our brain scans the world. The best way we have found to do this is through WWW journaling.

Before you start your practice or your round, write out the reminder, *My value comes from who I am, not from what I do.* Follow that with a growth mindset statement: *Anything that happens to me today is in my best interest and is an opportunity to learn and grow.* As you write down your score on each hole, write down at least two things you did well on that hole.

This exercise is usually very challenging when you first start doing it, but in time it gets easier because you consistently force your brain to scan the world differently. Remember, you have ignored what you have done well for a long time while blowing your "flaws" out of proportion. For the next six months, try and do the reverse. Let's ignore the flaws and focus on finding what you did well and how you got better.

After the round, write out two areas of growth. You only get two areas because it is hard to remember to focus on more than two at any one time. By writing down only two areas, you can look back at yesterday's journal and know exactly what you need to focus on today during training.

Finally, the last thing you write out is at least two things you learned, because nothing is a test. Everything is an opportunity to learn, but we need to focus on learning to actually get the benefits.

Focus on remedies, not faults.
—Jack Nicklaus

What Went Well Journaling

Hole 1: _____

Hole 2: _____

Hole 3: _____

Hole 4: _____

Hole 5: _____

Hole 6: _____

Hole 7: _____

Hole 8: _____

Hole 9: _____

Hole 10: _____

Hole 11: _____

Hole 12: _____

Hole 13: _____

Hole 14: _____

Hole 15: _____

Hole 16: _____

Hole 17: _____

Hole 18: _____

Post-Round

At least two things you learned:

_____

_____

_____

Two areas of growth:

_____

_____

Visit **www.t2bc.com/hack** for a printable WWW pin sheet journal, performance cue card, and good reminders.

CHAPTER 17

HOW DO YOU TALK TO YOURSELF?

I'm as guilty as anyone for blowing up and yelling on the golf course. The one thing you will never hear me do, though, is yell at myself.

If I talked to some people the way they talk to themselves, they would never be friends with me.

When someone I'm playing with starts yelling awful things at themselves, one of my favorite things to do is yell back, **"Hey! Don't talk to my friend like that**!"

It usually snaps them out of their self-deprecating state, giving them a chance to think about it. If you are going to have a blow-up moment, make sure you direct it externally rather than at yourself. I will cuss and yell, but never at myself. However, I work hard to not blow up like that because I've realized it just gives power to my opponents. But that is easier said than done.

I came up with the phrase "an opportunity for special" for Sam, but I've since incorporated into my own game. Instead of getting upset and saying things like "That is so unlucky!" or "I'm so screwed," we try and smile and say, **"This is an opportunity for special."**

The toughest moments and situations we find ourselves in on the course and in life truly are opportunities for special. If you were never in that position to begin with, then you can't do something special. This isn't some type of fake positivity. It is Truth. If Bubba Watson hadn't hit is ball into the trees, he never would have hit that remarkable slinging shot when he won *The Masters*.

Trouble is bad to get into but fun to get out of. If you're in trouble, eighty percent of the time there's a way out.
—Arnold Palmer

One thing I have found in playing and working with a lot of people is that the voice yelling at you is rarely your own. Typically, it is the voice of your father. It might be worth taking the time to figure out whose voice is yelling at you. Once we recognize it, we can start working to relinquish it and train ourselves to become our own best friend and coach. How would a great coach talk to you in those moments? Great coaches don't yell, demean, or shame. They encourage and constructively explain what to learn and what to do better next time. They have high standards and hold you to them, but only for what is 100 percent inside your control. We can only control our actions and the process, not the results.

If you want to tap into your fullest potential on and off the course, you've got to be intentional to become your own best friend and coach.

CHAPTER 18

LANGUAGE IS A FILTER TO MEANING

AN ANCIENT PROVERB says there is power of life and death in the tongue. Our words have immense power. The power to create and the power to destroy.

That is one of the reasons why I am so passionate about linguistic intentionality. It's why beneficial and constructive self-talk works. But it's also why we need to analyze the crazy games and rules we make up for ourselves.

Have you ever caught yourself saying things like this?

- "I had a terrible warm-up, and I always play bad after a terrible warm-up."
- "I never play well when I three-putt the first hole."
- "I always play bad when I play with slow players."
- "I always putt bad on slow greens" (the one I personally have to fight the most).

What rules are we creating: rules that benefit us or rules that trap us?

Are we giving away our power or harnessing it? *We get to make the rules.* No one else does!

Do you know how confusing and scary it is to play someone in golf that is bothered by nothing? As soon as I see someone who berates themselves, has terrible body language after a shot, or gets frustrated when they get a bad break, I know they are in for a very long day against me. The more things that bother them, the more I try and have a complete poker face and make it appear that nothing bothers me.

I used to drive people crazy when I would start workshops by telling them that their sport is stupid or silly. Then I would tell them that golf is stupid but still one of my favorite things to do.

Think about it: We hit a little white ball around a field and try and hit it into a tiny hole that is hundreds of yards away. If we don't do this as well as we expect, even though most of us barely spend any time practicing, we treat people terribly, including ourselves, and are miserable. When you really think about it logically and rationally, it doesn't make much sense. It is very silly and childish.

Here is the crazy thing. The more we keep golf in a healthy perspective, the better we will play. The more I realize that I am doing something very silly, the easier it is to allow my training to come through. The more I act as though my entire life depends on how I hit that little ball, the worse I'm going to play. When I tell people to surrender the outcome, I'm not advocating for them to act like they don't care. That's just another form of ego protection. *Rather, we are looking for the sweet spot of detaching ourselves and our self-worth from the outcome and simultaneously not relinquishing the effort or care of the things 100 percent inside our control.*

Language is a filter to meaning. No one gets to decide what something means except us. In tough moments, I try and remind myself, "*Thank you for the opportunity to compete.*"

One of the things that launched my professional career more than anything else was when I got knocked out over New Year's weekend after a night out in San Diego in 2015. After getting knocked out, I told myself, "This was in my best interest and an opportunity to learn and grow."

Was it painful? Absolutely. Was it embarrassing? Absolutely. But one of the most powerful things about being a human being is getting to decide what each experience means to you. How can you stop someone who truly believes that getting knocked out is in their best interest and an opportunity to learn and grow?! You can't.

Thomas Edison once had his entire laboratory and life's work go up in flames, yet with childlike joy, he told his son to go get his mother and all her friends to watch. His son objected, but Edison told him, "It's all right. We've just got rid of a lot of rubbish."[13]

Our perspective is our choice. Other people will try to tell us what things mean, but at the end of the day, only we get to decide.

This is why I came up with *True Mental Toughness* (TMT). John Wooden, the man voted the greatest coach of the twentieth century, said, "I've never met someone who described for me what you can do that is better than your best." I expanded on that, telling my clients that rather than focus on arbitrary outcome-based goals, they should focus on TMT. The way I defined TMT is: having a great attitude, giving your very very best, treating people really really well, and having unconditional gratitude—regardless of your circumstances.

In golf, we could substitute the last line with, "even when we are playing terrible golf and getting awful breaks."

If we focus on TMT instead of shooting a certain score or winning a tournament, we can only win. If we experience a hard day, we have an incredible opportunity to develop more TMT—the stuff everyone wants. Everyone wants people on their team—at home, in the office, on the course, or in business—that embody the characteristics of True Mental Toughness. The toughest moments become awesome opportunities to develop more TMT.

It's similar to what happens when I surrender a match or a hole. Once I surrender it, winning the hole or the match is just icing on the cake. It frees me up. Instead of feeling more pressure, I feel less. Instead of worrying, I get to have fun. Instead of raising my heart rate, my heart rate slows down.

---

13   Visit https://www.businessinsider.com/thomas-edison-in-the-obstacle-is-the-way-2014-5 for the full story.

Of course, I want to win! I'm a competitive freak. But I know that when I focus on TMT and surrender the outcome, I actually create the best opportunity to let my training and skill shine through and win. It is one of the strange paradoxes of life.

CHAPTER 19

NEW SCORECARD

THE SCORECARD SOCIETY judges us by is tragically flawed and pursuing it will leave you completely unfulfilled.[14]

Golf has a scorecard that we use, and if without being intentional, we can allow that card to have way too much power in our life. We created a tool that our clients found very helpful to combat this.

For those who don't play golf, we have them think about the two or three characteristics they most admire in others. Then we have them grade themselves twice a day on how they did with those characteristics. For golf we have expanded it a little bit, and golf always provides us with a great opportunity to develop more of the characteristics we want in our life.

T2BC New Scorecard for Golf*

Characteristic: _____

    Grade for the round: _____

Characteristic: _____

    Grade for the round: _____

How would you grade yourself on the following areas A+ to F?

    B&C Self-Talk: _____

    Perspective: _____

---

14 Quote from, *Chop Wood Carry Water.*

Powerful Body language: _____

Opportunity for special: _____

Swinging with conviction: _____

True Mental Toughness: _____

Course management: _____

Surrendering the outcome: _____

*These and other tools are available for download at www.t2bc.com/hack

CHAPTER 20

FORGED IN THE FIRE

WHEN I WOULD do workshops with college golf teams, one of the biggest challenges players told me they faced was a lack of confidence. Everyone was searching for that elusive feeling.

The problem with confidence is that it is a feeling, and feelings are fleeting. Some mornings you are going to feel confident, and other times you aren't going to have any confidence. We can start a round with this elusive feeling, only to see it leave and return many times. Sometimes we can lose that feeling for long periods of days, weeks, months, or years.

What's the lesson? If you can only play well when you feel confident, you are going to be in for a lot of trouble.

There's something more powerful than confidence: *conviction*. While confidence is a feeling, conviction is a belief deep within our hearts that doesn't change regardless of the circumstances. It is based on our track record and training.

The more that we do hard things, the more conviction we can develop.

In medieval times, a sword was a very important weapon. Swordsmiths took great care and pride in their craft. To start, they would take a large block of steel, one of the hardest materials on earth, and put it inside of a fire. The steel would heat up to a molten 2,000 degrees Fahrenheit. Then the swordsmith would take the red-hot steel out of the fire and start hitting it into form with a hard mallet.

The swordsmith could shape the sword until it cooled, but then the swordsmith would put it back into the fire to heat it again. To complete a sword, the swordsmith would repeat this process as many as twenty times before the sword was ready to cool for good.

Heat in the fire. Pound into shape.

Heat in the fire. Pound into shape.

Heat in the fire. Pound into shape.

The Japanese were pioneers in swordsmithing and called this process *shita-kitae.*

The best swords in the world were the ones that came out of the hottest fire and endured the most pounding. They were sharp, yet flexible enough to withstand blows. They were sturdy, yet light enough to carry in the field.

So many people want the edge and sharpness of a sword, but they don't want to go through the fire that will forge them. They *hope* to feel confident instead of spending time training in the toughest circumstances to actually prepare them for their moment.

Conviction comes from having been forged in the fire. *You cannot fake your way to conviction.* Facing tough circumstances head-on, conquering them, and remembering that you did is the only way to build true conviction.

Gaining conviction doesn't have to happen on the golf course either. My cold-water training, my sauna training, sleeping on skid-row, living in a homeless shelter for 7 months, living in the closet of a gym for 9 months, my work in the toughest housing projects training kids—all of these things helped build my conviction that I can do hard things, on or off the golf course. They build my conviction that I was built, not born, for tough moments.

When it comes to our training, we want to go into the fire on purpose. We want our training to be so challenging, scary, and hard that you know you are one of the best-trained golfers on the planet.

Remember the commercial in which Tiger Woods says, "There are no rainy days"? He is outside in the rain hitting balls. Where do you think his conviction on the course came from? Did you think he was born with it? No, he built it from a very young age through training.

The opportunity to become forged through fire is the greatest when the circumstances are the worst.

A wise person once said, *"Smooth seas do not make skilled sailors. Only consistently facing and conquering the rough seas will."*

When you feel uncertain and lonely, remember, *you can do hard things!*

When you feel out of your league, remember, *you can do hard things!*

When you feel like your back is against the wall, remind yourself, *I can do hard things!*

When I caddy for anyone, I try to remind the golfer to make every swing with "full conviction." When there is a debate about which club, or what type of shot to hit, I ask, "Which one can you hit with more conviction?"

What do you do when you don't "feel" like doing it?

We often think big decisions and big moments define our lives. Typically, though, it's the little decisions, added up and compounded over time, that impact our lives and who we become more than the big ones.

We obsess over the remarkable instead of simply doing the unremarkable with remarkable consistency. You don't need the most talent, money, equipment, or anything external. Just keep showing up, keep honing your craft, and keep getting back in the arena.

It's usually those who simply keep getting back up, dusting themselves off, and stepping back into the arena who win the long game.

Conviction comes from getting back into the arena over and over—even when you don't "have to." Conviction comes from doing hard stuff over and over again—even when you don't feel like it. Then when those storms of life hit, you know you can still operate with the deep conviction that only comes from doing hard stuff when you didn't feel like it.

Feelings are flaky. Conviction is what we want. But you can't buy it, and you can't fake it. Conviction can only be earned.

What little choices will you make today to earn that conviction when you need it most down the road?

> *Other golfers may outplay me from time to time, but they'll never outwork me.*
> ### —Tiger Woods

POUND THE STONE

A few people who read early drafts of this book wanted a more "prescriptive" approach to dropping their golf handicap. The truth is, I don't know which thing did it for me, and I don't think it was any one specific thing. I think it was the compound effect of everything I did.

I wrote an entire book, *Pound the Stone*, based on this poem by Jacob Reis:

> *When nothing seems to help, I go and look at a stonecutter hammering away at his rock perhaps a hundred times without as much as a crack showing in it. Yet at the hundred and first blow it will split in two, and I know it was not that blow that did it, but all that had gone before.*

I'm not a golf coach. Golf coaches can give you a prescription for how to get a better swing or golf IQ. For that, there is no one better than Sam. He has helped many of my "hack" friends improve their game, and he works with two of the best players in the world. No matter your current skill level, he will help you get better.

Most people have never had a playing lesson in their life, and in my opinion, they just waste time "working on their swing" on the range. You don't play golf on the range unless you are a long-drive competitor.

Everything is different on the course: how fast you swing, where you aim, where you set up on the tee box, what club you choose for the distance, when you decide to choke up, where you have the ball in your stance, and how you react to the hazards in front of you. A great coach needs to be there to guide you on how to play during a round. A great coach is also going to teach you all the other little things that go into managing your game well. There are lots of people who have beautiful swings on the range and on the course. But if they don't have a high golf IQ, then it doesn't matter how good their swing is. They are going to have a very hard time unleashing their full potential.

A few weeks ago, Sam and I were up in LA to play golf and see, Judah Smith. Sam talked with a guy who had recently become obsessed with golf, and he gave him a couple of skills to work on when we were chatting after church. The guy texted him the following week that it had added twenty-five yards to his driver. Sam is that good. I send all of my friends to him for *playing lessons*.

To improve your game, email Sam at samcyrgolf@gmail.com or message him on Instagram @samcyrgolf. I believe playing lessons are the best but he now has a program through the "skillest" app where he can work with you no matter where you are at in the world. [15]

The putting mat that I use is listed on Amazon as the SKLZ Vari-Break-adjustable putting green. I threw away the pads underneath and put the mat flat on the hardwood floor.

Books: As I mentioned a couple of times in this book, *Chop Wood Carry Water, Pound the Stone, Win in the Dark*, and *Burn Your Goals*, are all must-reads if you want to see how all the pieces of the mindset and heart posture perspective we teach fit together. Each book centers on teaching fables, except for *Burn Your Goals*.

Coaching and Mentorship: If you are interested in our T2BC mentorship program, you can visit our website at www.t2bc.com or email Lucas (lucas@traintobeclutch.com).

My Contact Info
Instagram: @realjoshuamedcalf
Twitter: @joshuamedcalf

---

15   There is a chance we will make a video course together in the future, so be on the lookout!

Cell: 918-361-8611 (Yes, this is my real phone number. I have two phones, but I respond to all the messages and calls personally.)
Email: joshua@traintobeclutch.com

THANK YOU'S

I am tremendously grateful to those who helped make this book better.

Andrew Downing and Ben Pellicani, your feedback from start to finish was incredibly helpful. This book wouldn't be what it became without you!

Scott Long and Rick Purcell, thank you for helping launch this book well!

Thank you, Fairway Golf and Jeff Fenstermacher, for always taking care of me.

Thank you, Yelyzaveta, for all your love and support through this season of my life and for the pictures from the club championship.

Thank you, Mom, for teaching me how to play sports and for all your love and wisdom. I still can't believe you thought there was no chance in the world that I *wouldn't* win that tournament when you arrived at my place that weekend. Your belief in me has always put wind in my sails. Thank you for being one of my shining stars.

Thank you, Amber, for being a rock in my life and always lifting me up when I am at the edge of the abyss. I know it's hard at times to have a best friend who is a manic-depressive, autistic artist.

Thank you, Lucas, for all your support and friendship. This wouldn't have been possible without you running the brand and letting me have a long sabbatical.

Thank you, Jim Willkie and all the guys at the club, for all the laughs and good times.

Printed in Great Britain
by Amazon

76828238R00073